TYRANT AND VICTIM
IN DOSTOEVSKY

D1454044

TYRANT AND VICTIM IN DOSTOEVSKY

by

Gary Cox

Slavica Publishers, Inc.
Columbus, Ohio

Slavica publishes a wide variety of books and journals dealing with the peoples, languages, literatures, history, folklore, and culture of the peoples of Eastern Europe and the USSR. For a complete catalog with prices and ordering information, please write to:

Slavica Publishers, Inc.
P.O. Box 14388
Columbus, Ohio 43214
USA

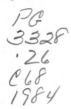

10/85

ISBN: 0-89357-125-3.

This book was published in 1984.

Text set by Randy Bowlus at the East European Composition Center, supported by the Department of Slavic Languages and Literatures and the Center for Russian and East European Studies at UCLA.

Printed in the United States of America.

ACKNOWLEDGMENTS

I gratefully acknowledge the people who have helped me work through the ideas and hone the style of this book. The list, presented here in alphabetical order, includes Slavists and non-Slavists, writers, friends and relatives:

Robert Belknap
Mary Parker Buckles
Joseph A. Caputo
Harold Cordry
Christine Leonard Cox
Miriam and Keith Cox
Clare Cross-Schmalbeck
James Curtis
Leslie Hermann
Bruce Keeling
Robert A. Maguire
Rufus W. Mathewson
Robin Miller
Daniel Orlovsky
James Peters
Rima Shore
Susan Siegel
George Smith

CONTENTS

CHAPTER 1

INTRODUCTION

Any reader who considers an author's fictional output as a whole confronts a situation very like that faced by an ethnologist who sets out to understand a primitive tribe. He encounters a population whose members interact with each other in a fashion quite peculiar to themselves, yet internally consistent, being prescribed by a set of unwritten rules. Literary criticism, like ethnology, tries to discover this set of rules and make it explicit, both for specialists and for the general reading public, thus clarifying the writer's (or the tribe's) view of humanity, and discovering patterns of behavior and thought which bring seemingly unrelated phenomena into a systematic whole.

When a writer's works are examined from the vantage point of another cultural tradition, this sense of ethnological exploration is heightened. The ethnic group provides a distinctive version of experience, emphasizing certain concepts at the expense of others, and the individual writer within that group gives a particularly distinctive slant on the nature of human behavior. Often a single concept, or a polarity between opposing concepts, will provide the key to understanding a unique vision of social interaction, organizing many of the writer's perceptions around a central axis. An understanding of this central axis enables readers and critics to see the author's work in clearer perspective.

In the novels of Fyodor Dostoevsky the concept of dominance in personal relationships provides such an axis around which human interaction is organized. If we examine the "population" which inhabits Dostoevsky's novels, we find that this microcosmic society is a rigidly structured hierarchy where power relationships are clearly defined and where behavior proceeds along lines suggested by the central concept of personal dominance. Of course, a strict concept of social hierarchy was characteristic of nineteenth century Russian society generally. By focusing upon this problem, Dostoevsky provides us with insight into the culture in which he lived. But the dominance hierarchy is not simply a Russian phenomenon. By concentrating much of his attention on this salient aspect of Russian culture, Dostoevsky gives us a brilliant, if occasionally eccentric, analysis of human behavior. The artistic structures he develops for dealing with this concept form one of the focal points of his artistic system.

Notes From the House of the Dead (1860–62), Dostoevsky's description of his years as a prisoner in a Siberian prison camp (1850–1854) have something of the character of an ethnological treatise. So rigidly separate were the classes in nineteenth century Russia that for an upper class intellectual from St. Petersburg to spend four years living with convicted criminals in Omsk was almost equivalent to his travelling to an aboriginal island to observe the behavior of the natives.[1] Yet what Dostoevsky found in Omsk was different mainly in degree, rather than in kind, from the bureaucratic and literary society of St. Petersburg which he had already recorded in his early stories and novellas. He found in Siberia a competitive hierarchy in which roles and behavior were determined by a rigid but unwritten code based on personal dominance and submission. He discovered that prisoners who were accustomed to assume command on the outside could be meek, docile, and even "womanish" with their superiors within the camp. (I 1) He found that they liked their officers to be stern and loved to discuss their rank. (I 8, II 5) But they compensated for this by bullying each other, setting up their own power hierarchy and exulting in their power over others. There were natural leaders who behaved much like foremen on a work crew, but if any man without this status gave a directive he was ridiculed for exceeding his station. (I 6) There were others who automatically assumed positions of servitude, who seemed ordained by destiny to wait upon others. (I 4, I 5)

Dostoevsky had seen this sort of thing before. As a young man *en route* to a St. Petersburg boarding school for the first time, Dostoevsky saw a government courier beating a coach driver, and noted that the driver responded by beating his horse. Writing of the scene years later, in *The Diary of a Writer,* Dostoevsky expanded the repercussions of the incident, moving down the pecking order. He imagined that the peasant driver's friends teased him, and that he again responded by attacking a creature lower than him in the dominance hierarchy, this time his wife.[2] (January 1876, III 1)

By the time of his imprisonment, Dostoevsky's early works had already exhibited a preoccupation with power hierarchies, derived to some extent from Gogol, Balzac, and other writers who dominated his early career. But in his early stories the writer dealt primarily with basic, uncomplicated types (with the exceptions of Mr. Golyadkin in *The Double* (1847) and Katerina and Murin in *The Landlady* (1847), in whom lay the seeds of future complexity). In "A Petersburg Chronicle," a series of early sketches for the *St. Petersburg News,* he described a self-important middle-aged bully preparing to marry a submissive young woman (April 27, 1847), he talked about the subservient toadies without whom men would "die of boredom" or else "gnaw at one another" (May 11), and he outlined the type of the weak, tender, even effeminate, young dreamer (June 15). All of these types reappeared frequently in his early stories and journalistic *feuilletons,* as did the type of the downtrodden copy-clerk, at the very bottom of the hierarchy, whom Dostoevsky inherited from Gogol and others. The interest in dominance hierarchies had already found expression prior to the Siberian experience.

But prison life added dimensions of profundity and complexity to the young Dostoevsky's understanding of power relationships. In prison Dostoevsky discovered that mixtures of these pure types, combinations of opposing extremes within single individuals, are the most interesting representatives of the power hierarchy. Here he met a sadistic major who was completely under the thumb of his orderly (I 2); he met a former smuggler, of colossal physical proportions, who was meek, quiet, and "lachrymose as a peasant woman" (I 1); he met a pious prisoner distinguished for his Bible reading who suddenly attacked an officer for no apparent reason. (I 2) Dostoevsky learned in prison that the inversion of the dominance hierarchy is often the mainspring of its operation, that the aggressor becomes a victim and the victim becomes an object of veneration. The most aggressive bully in prison, when his aggression resulted in a formal beating (administered by the prisoners themselves *en masse*), became something of a sacred being to his fellows. They would care for his wounds kindly, observing silence in a dimly candlelit barracks reminiscent of an orthodox sanctuary. (I 4) This treatment of the punished comrade echoes the position of the prisoners themselves in Russian society, where their murderous aggression had placed them in the position of victims. It also echoes the phenomenon of the scapegoat or sacrificial victim in primitive society, a chosen outcast who is first punished, and then venerated, by the group as a whole.[3]

A similar inversion of the dominance hierarchy may be discerned in the figure of the convict executioner. Selected for his physical strength, he receives special privileges and lives apart from the other convicts. But he becomes the supreme outcast of the group, viewed with an almost mystical terror by the other convicts. (II 3) Dostoevsky describes him thus: "He who has once experienced this power (*vlast*), this boundless dominion (*gospodstvo*) over the body, blood, and spirit of a man just like himself . . . thus becomes against his will powerless (*ne vlasten*) to control his sensation." The executioner's power, paradoxically, renders him powerless and causes him to be victimized as a social outcast. The perversion he embodies is viewed by Dostoevsky as a disease or a form of drunkenness, extremely dangerous to the body politic. Nor is it limited to the prison: "The characteristics of the executioner may be found in embryonic form in almost every contemporary person." (II 3) These are the characteristics Dostoevsky went on to study in his later fiction.

Many critics have noted Dostoevsky's preoccupation with these phenomena of personal dominance, but no one has produced a comprehensive and systematic study of the forms the dominance hierarchy takes in Dostoevsky's prose or of the means he proposes to neutralize the sado-masochistic aspects of the aggressive hierarchy. Andre Gide observes that Dostoevsky's hierarchies are based on degrees of pride and humility.[4] N. K. Mikhailovsky, in his essay "A Cruel Talent" (1882), written shortly after Dostoevsky's death in 1881, discusses at length the novelist's fascination with characters who delight in tormenting others or subjecting themselves to torment. Mikhailovsky notes that during Dostoevsky's early career his considerable talents were devoted to studying the psychology of the lamb being devoured by the wolf, while in his later career he turned to the psychology of the wolf. But most of Mikhailovsky's essay is given over to an attack on the preoccupation with gratuitous violence in Dostoevsky's works and on the sadistic proclivities which must have produced such an interest.[5]

The study presented in the following chapters will give a more dispassionate account of the paradigms of dominance and aggression in Dostoevsky's novels and the novelist's attempts to redeem the power hierarchy by inverting it. Some of the material here will cover ground already traversed by earlier critics, but the material will be organized with a view toward illuminating this particular set of themes.

Dostoevsky creates a language for dealing with the human personality by producing a set of stock types or stereotypical characters. The complex characters of his greatest works always transcend this character typology, but they are always rooted in it as well. The typology is a way of locating a character in a general behavioral framework. Individualized details of behavior and personality give the character a distinctive image without carrying him beyond the bounds of this type. Dostoevsky's most engaging characters take on a life of their own precisely because of their ability to surprise us with their unique attributes while remaining true to type.[6]

Let us look at the specific types of tyrants and victims encountered in the early and later works, and at the behavior patterns characteristic of them. First there is the predatory male, often a middle-aged man, who dominates women instinctively, if not always successfully, and who arouses the envy, and occasionally the rage, of his younger competitors. We typically see him preparing to marry a woman much younger than himself, usually the submissive type. We seldom see him in his role as an actual husband. He is a stock character and is rarely a central figure in the novels. Examples are

Mr. Bykov (Mr. Bull) of the writer's first novella, *Poor Folk* (1846), and Luzhin from *Crime and Punishment* (1866).

The second stock type is the submissive and sexually oppressed female. She is occasionally the consort of the man described above, and in later works she will often be forced into prostitution, although she never enjoys her work. Sonya in *Crime and Punishment* and Liza of *Notes from Underground* (1864), both forced into prostitution by family circumstances, are variants of this type, as is Varvara in *Poor Folk*.

This second group does undergo some development in the course of Dostoevsky's work, for in the middle and late novels these women often grow up to be members of the third group, the dominant females. One might say that they have upward mobility in the sexual hierarchy. The self-sufficient, dynamic women of the later novels (sometimes referred to as Dostoevsky's "infernal women") often have a history of early sexual abuse or humiliation at the hands of older men (Nastasya Filippovna in *The Idiot* (1868) and Grushenka in *The Brothers Karamazov* (1881)). The imperious dowagers found in almost all of the long novels form a sub-group among these dominant females.

The fourth group, the permanently low-ranking males, is quite varied, but all of the sub-types are related. This group begins with the lowly civil servant, represented by the downtrodden Makar Devushkin from *Poor Folk* (clearly an imitation of the hero of Gogol's "The Overcoat," Akaky Akakievich Bashmachkin). Next come the drunkards (often copy-clerks in their sober hours) like Marmeladov in *Crime and Punishment*. Cuckolded husbands comprise a third subtype, found in numerous short stories and in the novel *The Eternal Husband* (1870). Finally, there are the sycophantic buffoons, exemplified by the fawning and babbling Lebedev in *The Idiot*. Dostoevskian buffoonery is a somewhat more complex issue. Basically a self-destructive impulse in its inception, it can become an aggressive way of dealing with the world. Thus, like so many Dostoevskian gestures, it embraces both ends of the aggression-submission polarity. Several characters in the late novels, Fyodor Karamazov in *The Brothers Karamazov* and Stepan Verkhovensky in *The Devils,* display some features of the buffoon but actually belong in other categories. Lebedev's buffoonery is mitigated by his interpretation of the apocalypse, an important and serious issue in *The Idiot*. Still, on the whole, the buffoons belong in this category of low-ranking males. These low-ranking male characters are objects of derision or compassion (sometimes both) in Dostoevsky's novels, but their one-dimensionality usually prevents them from becoming the focus of the most serious psychological study.

The dreamer, another character type standard in Dostoevsky's early works, requires more explanation. This is an intelligent and good-natured young loner who relates awkwardly to other men. The dreamer envies his more imposing peers, but he dares not compete with or even emulate them. The young hero of *White Nights* (1848), where the term "dreamer" is first used, calls himself "neuter" and compares himself with a kitten, tortured by children, who hides under a chair. He emerges from his hiding place during the bright summer nights of St. Petersburg and wanders about the city watching other people, thinking, dreaming. His romantic dream is of a pure love for a woman who is married to a gloomy older man. The husband torments them both and they fear him like timid children. The older man is both rival and role-model. Of course triangular relationships of this sort have important literary antecedents in Rousseau's *Julie, ou la nouvelle Heloise* and Goethe's *Die Leiden des jungen Werthers,* both of which are important for Dostoevsky's work generally. This fantasy, which René Girard has called "the dream of life by threes" (*le rêve de la vie à trois*),[7] is briefly realized in the short novel *The Landlady.* The younger dreamer does not exactly disappear from Dostoevsky's later works, but rather re-emerges, transformed after a decade or so, as the psychopathic hero of Dostoevsky's middle period.

The Dostoevskian psychopath begins where the dreamer does, alienated from the society of men because, in his insecurity about his personal identity, he dares not define himself as part of that society. Cut off from others, he becomes absorbed completely in his own internal reality. Like a philosophical solipsist, who denies the reality of the world outside his own mind, the Dostoevskian psychopath is unable to deal with the world beyond himself. He becomes an "emotional solipsist." But the psychopath goes further than the dreamer. The dreamer, feeling rejected by society, or, more precisely, having rejected himself on behalf of society, responds only passively, but the psychopathic character responds aggressively. He is obsessed by the dominance hierarchy, and he behaves sadistically toward those beneath him and masochistically toward those above him. Knowing only the extrmees of power-related behavior, he takes equal delight in aggressive domination of others and submissive self-humiliation at the hands of others. The fullest expression of this pathological type is found in the unpleasant narrator of *Notes from Underground,* but elements of this personality are found throughout Dostoevsky's middle and late works.

If all of Dostoevsky's characters were portrayed as stereotypically as is suggested above, his work would constitute merely a gallery of cartoon portraits, like the one found in Gogol's works. But Dostoevsky does not stop here. Working with a set of stock characters, he manipulates and recombines their features, producing out of these stereotyped elements a profound analysis of human behavior. Some of Dostoevsky's most enigmatic characters combine features from both extremes of the dominance/submission polarity. It is not that they merely fall between the two extremes; that would make them ordinary people. Rather, they maintain within themselves a tension between the unmitigated extremes of dominance and submissiveness. Stavrogin in *The Devils* (*The Possessed,* 1872) and Versilov in *A Raw Youth* (1875) are men endowed by nature with extraordinary personal strength and charisma, and yet strange stories circulate about the public humiliations each has undergone. These unsynthesized oppositions heighten the mystical aura which surrounds both men. Such combinations of opposing qualities are not unique to the late works, although they are more frequently found there. Characters like Valkovsky (*The Insulted and the Injured,* 1862) and even Murin (*The Landlady,* 1847) display similar conflicting characteristics. In the rough drafts for *The Idiot* such an unresolved internal opposition finally split a proposed character into two in the final version of the novel. It is apparent that the aggressive Rogozhin and the passive Myshkin were conceived as a single contradictory character. The final result is a pairing of the two characters in which their identification with each other is based on opposition. This sort of character-doubling produces a strong bond of friendship and hostility and a suppressed consciousness of performing an act of destiny together. The pair will be discussed at greater length in Chapter 5.

These stereotypical elements produce a language for portraying human interaction, a language which is most revealing when its elements are combined in unexpected ways. Even in his best works, most notably *The Brothers Karamazov,* where Dostoevsky transcends the stereotypical approach almost completely, it is clear that he is still working with the same language. Differences in degree and type of dominance form the basis of this language; hence these distinctions constitute an important key to Dostoevsky's view of the human personality.

As suggested above, inversions of the established power structure are crucial in Dostoevsky's work. In fact, such power inversions become the structural center of many of the mature works. A character who is passive, weak, or low-ranking in the power hierarchy, characterized by spiritual rather than physical power, often achieves moral, or even physical ascendancy in the pivotal events of the novel. This sort of reversal takes place, for instance, between the underground man and his prostitute, Liza (*Notes from Underground*), between the murderer Raksolnikov and his meek girlfriend Sonya (*Crime and Punishment*), and between the aggressive Rogozhin and the Christlike Myshkin (*The Idiot*).

In dramatizing these inversions, Dostoevsky again uses a set of stock elements, certain incidents or behavior patterns which recur with almost obsessive regularity in his works. J. M. Meijer has called this technique "situation rhyme" and has perceptively outlined its structural importance in *Crime and Punishment*. He notes that certain details continually recur in otherwise unrelated scenes and in connection with different characters. Examples include the numerous discussions of the resurrection of Lazarus, doors locked from the inside, suicide (or the contemplation of it) from a bridge, to mention only a few. Meijer limits his discussion to *Crime and Punishment* and opines that the device probably originated with that novel.[8]

In fact, however, the technique is not limited to any one work or even one period in Dostoevsky's career. Situation rhyme ties together all of Dostoevsky's works (and the rough drafts for them) in an interconnected web of recurrent imagery and obsessive behavior paradigms. Indeed the much discussed phenomenon of character doubling may be seen as a type of situation rhyme. Ralph Matlaw has documented the recurrence of two important images, insects and child rape, throughout the body of Dostoevsky's works.[9] Other examples abound, as the following pages will demonstrate.

A behavior paradigm related to the power inversion is the dramatic bow. This paradigm assumes particular importance, as Meijer notes, in *The Brothers Karamazov* (but it is also important in *The Devils* and *Crime and Punishment*). Father Zosima's bow to Dmitry introduces the theme and the bows of Katya and Dmitry to each other are crucial background materials. Another related behavior paradigm found in many of the novels is the scene of public humiliation. In *Notes from Underground* the hero dreams with horrified fascination of being forcibly evicted from the male peer group by his mocking fellows, and then by his obnoxious behavior succeeds in realizing this nightmare several times. In this work, and even as early as *White Nights,* the possibility of such public humiliation is symbolized by the image of an animal being tortured by humans (an image which finds its most forceful and significant dramatization in Raskolnikov's dream of the horse being beaten in *Crime and Punishment*). In later novels the paradigm of public humiliation becomes more specific and usually takes one of two forms: the public slap (*The Idiot, The Devils, A Raw Youth,* and numerous references in rough drafts and notebooks from the 1870's) or cowardice in a duel (*The Devils,* "A Gentle Creature," *The Brothers Karamazov*). These behavior paradigms reinforce a central structural principle of Dostoevsky's most important works, the inversion of the dominance hierarchy.

In fact the power inversion, symbolized by bowing, is not only an important structural principle, it is also a crucial element in Dostoevsky's moral system, particularly when the aggressor identifies with his victim (*Crime and Punishment*), or when the compassion produced by guilt provides a bridge between the psychopathic character and the world, releasing him from his solipsistic isolation.

The passive victim has mystical power in Dostoevsky, or to preserve the ethnological analogy, we may say that the victim has totemic force or *mana* in this body of literature. The crime against the totemic victim is the worst imaginable, but when that crime is enacted in a ritual way the aftermath is salvation. In Dostoevsky's last novel, *The Brothers Karamazov,* two parallel murders point up the ritual aspect of this redemptive drama. The novel contains two groups of adolescent men, each of which causes a death. The "murder" of the totemic victim, Ilyusha Snegiryov, and the murder of old Fyodor Karamazov, his opposite in the dominance hierarchy, both produce a sense of personal guilt in the groups of young men who commit them, and this social conscience serves as a basis for adult interaction.

Father Zosima in *The Brothers Karamazov* finally embodies the system of religious ethics which results from this ritual drama. The central image of Zosima's system is that of the master bowing to the servant. When the weak character bows to the strong, although he achieves thereby a degree of moral ascendancy, in the final analysis he only continues and exacerbates the sado-masochistic features of the power structure. By contrast, when the strong man wilfully and consciously bows to the weak, as does Father Zosima, the perversions inherent in the dominance hierarchy are neutralized and dispersed. Christ's washing of his disciples' feet is a relevant subtext for these situations, illustrating the way in which the aggression-submission pattern intersects the network of religious imagery in Dostoevsky's work. The solution to the aggression problem, for Dostoevsky, is inherent in the structure of hierarchical relationships, and is achieved through a restructuring of their components, through an inversion of the hierarchy.

A synopsis of one of Dostoevsky's novels will give substance to the phenomena outlined above and will make clear how the power axis works in a Dostoevsky novel. It should not be a synopsis of one of the major masterpieces, however, for they transcend the stereotypical approach and concentrate on one or two aspects of the dominance structure rather than presenting the whole. *A Raw Youth,* on the other hand, while it is the least successful of Dostoevsky's long novels, embodies virtually all of the characters and behavior patterns discussed above in a very stereotypical way; in

fact it fails precisely because it tries to do too much. As a result it is confused, uncentered, and reads like an unpolished draft from Dostoevsky's
notebooks. For that very reason, however, it will serve our immediate purpose admirably. The patterns which will emerge from an examination of *A
Raw Youth* may then be traced in Dostoevsky's greater novels.

The young hero Arkady Dolgoruky is a classic example of the emotional
solipsist. At one point he actually expresses doubts about the existence of
the world outside himself. He is the illegitimate son of an artistocrat and a
submissive serf woman, hence the imagery of parental tyranny becomes
fully literal: he is his father's slave. His feelings toward his father are a
complex mixture of hatred, envy and adoration characteristic of the Dostoevskian psychopath's attitude toward his hated rival. Versilov, the father,
is a mystifying combination of overwhelming strength and the will to self-
humiliation (his name suggests a combination of "faith" and "strength");
he is a less successful version of Stavrogin from *The Devils*. Verislov's drive
toward self-debasement is illustrated by three incidents: a secret marriage
to a consumptive halfwit, a mysterious relationship with a young woman in
distress (for which the motive is either highly noble or utterly base, but
which in any case results in her suicide), and a report that he publicly
recieved a slap from a younger man but did not respond to the challenge
with a duel.

Dolgoruky's schoolboy experiences involved him in a competition he
could not win, since he was attending an aristocratic boarding school where
his illegitimacy was known. His hostile relations with his schoolfellows
remind one of *Notes from Underground.* One of the only school chums who
has remained a friend is the sadistic bully Lambert, who used to beat Dolgoruky and whose current specialty is the sexual humiliation of women.
There is also a weak-willed young rake, Prince Sokolsky, who seduces Dolgoruky's sister and fathers a child by her, a nihilistic student named Kraft
(German "power"), and the hero's legal father, Makar Dolgoruky, an itin-
erant pilgrim who wanders about preaching a gospel which anticipates
Father Zosima's in *The Brothers Karamazov.*

The structural center of the novel (if it can be said to have a center) is the
passion both father and son feel for the imperious and beautiful Katerina
Nikolaevna Akhmakova. Versilov's feeling for her is a consuming and irrational romantic passion, while Dolgoruky's is a very strong adolescent
crush, heightened by his knowledge of his father's passion. This displaced
Oedipal competition produces as much cameraderie as hostility between
father and son, and it echoes the fascination with the *ménage à trois* evident
as early as *White Nights.* (Turgenev's *First Love* is quite relevant here, as it

involves a similar Oedipal competition.) Dolgoruky has in his possession a letter potentially ruinous to Akhmakova and it is the power which this letter confers upon him, power over Akhmakova and over his father, which is designed to sustain the reader's interest throughout the novel. Finally, the letter is produced in a scandalous climactic scene which occasions a great deal of running about and shouting, but which does not really change anything. It does seem at least to exhaust Versilov, who is seen recovering in the epilogue, and to placate Dolgoruky.

What can this grab-bag of a novel tell us about Dostoevsky's great masterpieces? Here all of the pieces of the Dostoevskian jigsaw lie on the table before us, some of them unassembled, others artlessly forced together with a heavy hand. But at least they are all here. Dostoevsky's "language" of stock characters and incidents is fully displayed. Elsewhere, where the art is greater, the picture is less complete, for the great novels rise above the stereotypical system. It remains for the critic, in the chapters which follow, to lay bare the system to which both these stock elements and their more sophisticated recombinations belong, and show how that system operates as a hidden mainspring in Dostoevsky's great masterpieces.

This complex of ideas and images in Dostoevsky's work has been written about in bits and pieces, but never seen whole. Its importance, and its component parts, can be understood in a new perspective if we view it as a unified and coherent system. This system, the tyrant-victim paradigm, is one of the fundamental structures which informs Dostoevsky's work. The other structures, clusters of imagery relating to religious, psychological, social, familial and other themes, overlap with it and with each other. An understanding of the tyrant-victim problem in Dostoevsky's work will illuminate these other related systems of imagery and provide an important key to Dostoevsky's understanding of the human condition.

CHAPTER 2

BONDING HIERARCHIES IN LITERATURE
BEFORE DOSTOEVSKY

The previous chapter opened with an analogy comparing literary analysis to ethnological study, the study of primitive social systems. But this analogy may be pushed back to the even more basic level of ethology, the branch of biology that studies the interaction of individual organisms and the structure of animal groups. One of the most important areas of study in ethology is the examination of the dominance hierarchy as a basic structure in animal societies.

On the boundary between these two nearly homonymous sciences, anthropologist Lionel Tiger has examined male bonding in human societies from an ethological perspective. Tiger's book, *Men in Groups,* is important for our purposes, for here we see the operation of the human dominance hierarchy, the subject matter of Dostoevsky's novels, at its most basic level. Tiger uses the term "male bonding" to describe the ties between group members which clarify dominance relationships and reinforce the sense of group membership. He notes that, even in non-human primate societies, male bonding seems to be strongest in species where dominance ranking is important and intra-group aggression is prevalent. According to this view, in order for early human groups to survive, the bond was necessary to inhibit aggression against the dominant individuals who were so important to the maintenance of group structure. Subdominant individuals needed to suppress aggression upward in the hierarchy, and yet they had to have the capacity to exert dominance within a limited sphere or to assume control at a later date.[1]

The bonds which performed these functions not only prevented the dissolution of the group, but actually enhanced its cohesion. Young males would seek validation through attachment to superiors and peers, and this led to the establishment of membership prerequisites and a strengthening of group feeling. Looking to each other for status, bonding males could present a corporate self to the larger community. The loyalties thus produced formed the backbone of the community, producing what may have been the first instances of guilt, another factor in group cohesion.[2]

Deformations of this hierarchy, dramatic shifts within it, and competitive relationships between two of its members, are frequent topics in literature. It is not Dostoevsky's interest in these bonding hierarchies as such that makes him unique. What distinguishes him in the literary tradition is the central importance that such hierarchies assume in his work and the frequent recurrence of certain patterns of shift within the hierarchy. The most interesting literary characters are often those who strive to produce change in the hierarchy. Tiger calls such individuals "charismatic."[3] The "charismatic" inversion of the dominance hierarchy is the central paradigm of Dostoevsky's literary works.

But Dostoevsky was by no means the first writer to deal with bonding hierarchies in literature. His interest in these issues was formed to a considerable extent by the writers he read. The treatment of male bonding and the dominance hierarchy by Pushkin, Lermontov, Gogol and Balzac provide important antecedents to Dostoevsky's work. It will be helpful first to deal with several crucial works by those writers before moving on to the analysis of Dostoevsky's own works.

Pushkin's Belkin tales are five short stories parodying various themes of Romanticism. The first of them, "The Shot," takes on the conventions of dueling literature, and all of the action is produced by the struggle for status in the male bonding group. The hero, Silvio, has all the morose manners and mysterious past of the most typical of Byronic heroes. Although retired from military life, he lives in an isolated military outpost, devoid of high society and even feminine companionship. the regimental officers, all considerably his junior, look upon him with adolescent awe:

> He was about thirty five, so we looked up to him as an old man. His experience gave him a good deal of authority over us, and furthermore, his habitual gloom, his severe manner of life and his evil tongue strongly influenced our young minds. (I)

In fact this sort of leadership of a pack of respectful younger males seems to be just the sort of situation Silvio craves and seeks out, for we soon discover that this sort of thing was characteristic of his earlier life as well. He tells the narrator:

> I am accustomed to having the ascendancy, but in my youth this was a passion with me. In our time rowdiness was in fashion, and I was the number one hell-raiser in the army. We bragged of drunkenness, and I outrank the famous Burtsov. . . . My comrades worshipped me. . . . (I)

The all important duel takes place, then, when Silvio's position as leader of the pack is challenged. When the challenger comes on the scene, it is Silvio's own description that we hear, and his admiration is considerable. He describes the man in glowing terms as a paragon of all the virtues he himself holds dear. The challenger proffers friendship, but Silvio rejects it. He can only be friends with underlings; an equal, however admired, is a rival:

My primacy was shaken. Lured by my reputation, he began to seek my friendship, but I received him coldly and he backed away from me without any regret. I came to hate him. His successes in the regiment and with women drove me to absolute despair. I began to seek occasions to quarrel with him. (I)

The emotions of admiration, envy, and hatred are pathologically confused in Silvio.

Silvio is upset because he can do nothing which will affect this young man and thus exhibit his power over him. The young man is unmoved by the prospect of facing Silvio's shot, so Silvio cuts short the duel, reserving his shot until such time as the young man will perceive the full force of Silvio's control over his life.

Years later Silvio achieves full gratification of his wishes by dangling his rival over the precipice of death in the presence of the latter's hysterical young wife. It is significant that both use the respectful form of address in the first duel, while in the continuation of the duel Silvio uses the familiar forms as a way of underlining his ascendancy over his opponent, especially since the latter retains the polite form and even calls Silvio "sir." (II) Here it becomes absolutely clear that the shot is important to Silvio only as a means of establishing and displaying his control over his rival:

> 'I will not shoot,' replied Silvio. 'I am satisfied. I have seen your agitation, your fear. I forced you to shoot at me. I have achieved what I wished. You will remember me.' (II)

Silvio is a man consumed by the need to dominate other men, and as we will see in the later chapters of this book, he comes to represent one extreme of human behavior in Dostoevsky's work.

A similar but more complex personality is Pechorin in Lermontov's *A Hero of Our Time.* We first hear of Pechorin through Maksim Maksimych, his former commanding officer, who behaves more like a faithful and adoring puppy whenever Pechorin is around. The most important section of the novel, "Princess Mary," is concerned with Pechorin's activities at a fashionable spa in the Caucasus. The plot relies heavily on fortuitous coincidences and nefarious conspiracies which are overheard. But several aspects of Pechorin's attitudes toward other characters and toward himself are crucial as preludes to certain concerns in Dostoevsky's works. Once again the hero's relations with a group of young military officers is central to the action but here Pechorin is an outcast from that group rather than a leader in it. What is more, he despises the group and takes pride in his status as an outcast. His need for supremacy has gone to such lengths that he will not even deign to be a member of the group, and he finally humiliates the group in the novel's *denouement.*

Like Silvio, Pechorin sees friendship as a relationship based on power, but he is unwilling to exert the effort required to achieve such dominance over other men:

> . . . I have no talent for friendship. One of the two friends is always the slave of the other, although often neither of them will admit this to himself. I cannot be a slave, but to take command in such a situation is a tiresome task, since it must be accompanied by deceit. Besides, I have enough lackeys and money. (May 13)

Power over women comes more easily to Pechorin:

> I have never become the slave of a woman I loved; on the contrary, I have always acquired an invincible power over their wills and hearts without even trying. (May 16)

He satisfies his lust for personal dominance in romantic relationships:

> There is boundless pleasure in the possession of a young soul, barely unfolded to the world! . . . Ambition is nothing other than a thirst for power, and my greatest satisfaction is to subjugate to my will everything that surrounds me. To arouse a feeling of love, devotion and fear toward myself—isn't that the primary sign and the greatest triumph of power? (June 3)

Pechorin continues along these lines for some time, sounding quite like Dostoevsky's underground man in his relations with the prostitute Liza. (See Chapter 3)

Pechorin delights in arousing the feelings of love and hatred in others while experiencing no emotion himself. His avoidance of the melodramatic passions is heralded by his replay, in French, to Grushnitsky, his rival in love, early in the "Princess Mary" section of the novel:

> My dear man, I despise women in order to avoid loving them, for other-wise life would be too ridiculous a melodrama. (May 11)

This staged witticism, along with Grushnitsky's epigram which calls it forth, acts as a fairly accurate key to character. The key concepts from these phrases, love, contempt, and hatred, are used consistently throughout the remainder of the section to define the melodramatic and analytical character types represented by Grushnitsky and Pechorin respectively.[4]

Pechorin's self-analysis results in a division of his personality into two *personae*, an actor and an observer:

> For a long time I have lived, not by my heart, but by my head. I weigh
> and analyze my own passions and acts with stern curiosity, but without
> involvement. There are two men within me: one lives in the full sense of
> that word, the other cogitates and judges him. (Conclusion)

At the climax of the work, when Pechorin is overtaken by the despised
melodramatic passions, the second *persona* becomes a hypothetical observer
who looks upon Pechorin as he himself looks upon others:

> For a long time I lay motionless and wept bitterly, making no effort to
> restrain my tears and wailing. . . . My soul was deprived of its strength,
> my reason fell silent, and if anyone had seen me at the moment he would
> have turned away in contempt. (Conclusion)

Pechorin's self-analysis, his "intensified self consciousness," as Dostoevsky's underground man would call it, produces a division of the personality
into self and other which eventually results in contempt for the self.
Pechorin says in a diary entry, "I sometimes despise myself. . . . Is this not
why I despise others as well?" (June 14) He even succeeds in partially
infecting the melodramatic Grushnitsky with this attitude. Grushnitsky's
last words are "I despise myself, and I hate you." (Conclusion)

It is not many steps from Pechorin to the underground man. Strip
Pechorin of his swashbuckling exterior, his good looks, and his success in
the *grand monde,* and one finds an essential personality structure quite like
that of Dostoevsky's anti-hero.[5] His desire for personal power over others
is central to his psychological makeup. All of his relationships, both with
men and with women, are deformed by this central concern for dominance.

The kind of self-analysis which is so destructive in Pechorin's character
was to become a basic feature of the most important literary characters
during the great age of psychological realism in Russia. Dostoevsky's
underground man calls such self-consciousness a disease. Turgenev describes it (as does the underground man) as the source of indecisiveness and
inactivity in his analysis of the "Hamlet" type in Russian literature. Finally,
Tolstoy's troubled heroes, Pierre Bezukhov, Andrey Bolkonsky and Kon-
stantin Levin partake deeply of such self-analysis.

Of course Pechorin is also a version of the Byronic hero, and his cynicism
and lust for power have an established precedent in the Romantic period.
But the particular form these traits take in Pechorin, self analysis and consequent self hatred, while they are outgrowths of Romanticism, also herald
the direction in which psychological realism was to move. Pechorin forms
an important link between the Byronic heroism of the early nineteenth century and the psychopathology which lies at the core of Dostoevsky's work.

When we move from Lermontov's novel to the comic stories of Gogol, we feel that we are stepping into an utterly different world, yet the issues addressed are sometimes similar. The issue of competition in an all male peer group is crucial in Gogol's story "The Nose," as in "The Shot" and *A Hero of Our Time,* but in Gogol's comic story male status and identity are conferred by the possession of foolish external symbols.

St. Petersburg in the early nineteenth century was a highly structured bureaucratic hierarchy based on Peter the Great's table of ranks, which provided a hierarchical structure for the civil service. But in Gogol's comic St. Petersburg, competition in the bureaucratic world is parallelled by, and confused with, competition in a sexual hierarchy, where status is conferred on the basis of competitive public exhibition of facial hair. The absurd emphasis on the grooming and display of moustaches and sideburns as a sign of masculine status underlies the phallic character of the nose. When the hapless hero Kovalyov wakes up one morning with his nose mysteriously missing, the catastrophe is devastating to his male ego.

As is so often the case in Gogol's works, characters are described in terms of a single physical feature which comes to represent the whole person. For male characters in this story, that feature is always a nose, mustache, or sideburns, and it is always indicative of that character's masculine authority or status. The police officer who interrogates the barber early in the story has "a noble appearance, with broad sideburns, a three-cornered hat and a sabre. . . ." and he strikes terror into the barber's heart. The barber tires to mollify the policeman by offering to shave him, but the latter informs him that three barbers already consider it an honor to shave him. His "nobility" is evidenced not only by the imposing appearance of his sideburns, but by the number of lower ranking men that are honored to tend them. When he appears later he is again described in terms of his handsome sideburns, and in this passage his wife and children are mentioned several time with no apparent purpose except to stress his potency.

This policeman is so well placed in the male hierarchy that he pays no heed to the qualifications of those beneath him:

> I'm nearsighted, and if you stand right in front of me, I'll see only that you've got a face, but I won't see your nose or your beard or anything else. (II)

A similarly imposing figure is the doctor:

> . . . a fine looking man, who had marvelous sideburns black as pitch, a healthy, fresh wife, ate fresh apples in the morning, and kept his mouth extraordinarily clean. . . . (II)

Note that the beard and the wife are mentioned in the same breath, as though they were objects of the same order. This is a typical Gogolian humorous device, and here it underscores the connection between facial hair and masculine potency.

Men who rank low in the masculine bonding hierarchy are noted for the slovenly appearance of their beards and moustaches. Ivan Yakovlevich, the barber, who makes his living grooming other men, is himself never shaven, and his collar is old and shiny. (I) Collars and uniform buttons (indicating bureaucratic status) are also signs of masculine prowess here, probably because of their proximity to the all important nose.

Before losing his nose, Kovalyov is the kind of man who loves to strut down Nevsky Avenue exhibiting his finely groomed whiskers:

> Major Kovalyov was accustomed to taking a walk along Nevsky Avenue every day. His shirt collar was always extremely clean and heavily starched. His sideburns were of the sort that may be seen even these days on local or provincial surveyors, architects and regimental doctors, also on men who carry out various police duties and in general on all men who have chubby rosy cheeks and play a good hand of boston. These sideburns go along the very center of the cheek and right on up to the nose. (II)

The nose is the centerpiece of all this masculine regalia, and it is easy to see why a man like Kovalyov is upset when, inspecting his nose for blemishes before his morning constitutional, he discovers it to be missing.

That the nose is a genital symbol is clear not only from the attention to other symbols of masculine potency, but also from the repeated assertion that the nose is the most important organ to a *man*, particularly to a man of some status:

> If I had an arm or a leg missing, that would be better. Or if I had no ears—that would be pretty rotten, but still it would be easier to bear. But a man without a nose—the devil knows what he is, neither fish nor fowl, not a proper citizen, just something to take and chuck out the window. (II)

But a nose, it appears, is not particularly important for a woman to have. Walking past a row of beggar women, Kovalyov meditates as follows:

> Of course, I . . . well, I'm a major. For me to go about without a nose, one must agree, is indecent. For some tradewoman or other, who sells cleaned oranges on Voskresensky bridge, it's all right to sit there without a nose, but I've got prospects of . . . Besides, I'm acquainted with ladies in many homes. . . . (II)

Not only is a nose more essential to a man than to a woman, but it is essential precisely because he has relations with women. Kovalyov says to a newspaper clerk, when placing an advertisement to retrieve his nose:

> Judge for yourself, how can I remain without such a noticeable part of my body, really? It's not as though it were some little toe or other, so that inside my boot no one could see it missing. On Thursdays I go to the home of the wife of the State Councilor Chekhtaryov. Palegeya Grigorevna Podtochina, a staff officer's wife, and her very pretty daughter, are also particular acquaintances of mine, and you judge for yourself, how can I now . . . I can't make an appearance there now. (II)

Again and again in the course of his search to recover his nose, Kovalyov begins to flirt, or think about flirting, with a pretty woman, but then breaks off when he remembers that he has no nose. The implication is clearly that without a nose it would be senseless to enter into relations with a woman.

After recovering his nose Kovalyov's reaction is twofold: he is competitive with men, staring down with pleasure an officer who has a small nose, while in front of women he is simply exhibitionistic, stuffing his wayward nose elaborately and painstakingly full of snuff in front of Podtochina and her daughter. (III)

Gogol's story is pure froth in one sense, for the premise is not only impossible but idiotic. But the hierarchical patterns of human interaction here form a humorous counterpart to the bonding hierarchies already noted in Pushkin and Lermontov, patterns which were to become a basis for the more serious study of human relationships in Dostoevsky's works. We need not assume that the sexual features of the above interpretation were explicitly accepted by Dostoevsky in order to see that the bonding hierarchies they support form a basis for certain elements in his own work. Indeed, the sexual dimensions of the bonding hierarchy are seldom explicit, or even conscious, in daily interactions based on that hierarchy. The male characters in "The Nose" construct and validate their concepts of their own identity and worth in competition with one another on the basis of silly external symbols. The result is a competitive hierarchy of masculine rank which, although satirized here, corresponds to similar patterns in Dostoevsky's novels.

At least one non-Russian writer must be included in the literary prehistory of Dostoevsky's concern for bonding hierarchies. Dostoevsky's first publication was a translation of Balzac's *Eugenie Grandet,* and his interest in the French novelist continued throughout his career. Balzac's view of society as an enormous ladder certainly colored Dostoevsky's emerging ideas.

Balzac, like Dostoevsky, is interested in depicting extremes of character. His positive characters, as Donald Fanger has observed, are sentimentalized victims, while his evil characters are predatory devils.[6] Leonid Grossman maintained that Eugenie Grandet was the prototype for Dostoevsky's meek women.[7]

But there are important differences in outlook between the two writers. In Balzac's world one senses a petrified system of political and social hierarchies rather than the natural dominance of one human being over another through personal charisma. Balzac even speaks of society as though it were stratified rock: "human beings are packed in strata, layer above layer, in the framework of society."[8] In this sense the hierarchies of Balzac and Gogol show more affinity, while Dostoevsky's treatment of personal dominance is closer to that of Pushkin and Lermontov.

The great tools of power in Balzac's world are money and scandalous knowledge. Alliances are made and broken, social battles fought and won on the basis of these two great principles. They appear in Dostoevsky's works as well, but they turn out to be secondary to the power of dominant personalities. The money Dmitry gives Katya in *The Brothers Karamazov,* for instance, gives him a moment of voluptuous power over her, but the paradoxical power of her submission to him makes him an insect before her in the long run. This too comes to be symbolized by money, but the personal relationship is primary. Likewise in Part I of *The Idiot,* the large bundle of money which Nastasya Filippovna throws into the fire is interesting primarily because of the way it illustrates the power relationships between Nastasya, Ganya, Rogozhin, and Myshkin. A bundle of money alone could hardly produce such an electrifying scene in Dostoevsky's works. Rather, the money augments the excitement produced by personal relationships. Even scandalous secrets are not primary in Dostoevsky. They are either supplementary to the main action (*Crime and Punishment, The Brothers Karamazov*) or they fail to produce the intended excitement (*A Raw Youth*).

In Balzac and Dostoevsky we seem to be witnessing the dominance hierarchy at different stages of development. Balzac presents a well developed code of hierarchical relationships through which even personal charisma cannot break. Dostoevsky brings us to a more basic level where the naked power of a strong personality over a weak one cuts across social structures and forms a basis for hierarchical relationships.

Occasionally Balzac foreshadows Dostoevsky's concern for this more basic type of power, most clearly in the relationship between Vautrin and Rastignac in *Old Goriot.* The physical description of the undisguised Vautrin is a combination of naturalistic details and Romantic cliches of personal charisma:

> The short, brick-red hair lent a shocking suggestion of strength combined with cunning to the face; the whole head gave an impression of power in harmony with the powerful chest and shoulders, and at the moment the soul and spirit of the man were apparent in his face, as if he stood in a lurid glare thrown by the flames of Hell. (219)

Like Dostoevsky's Rogozhin (*The Idiot*), Vautrin's personal charisma is conveyed in "the blood-congealing, mesmeric look that certain men of outstanding magnetic power possess the seret of." (211) This is another Romantic cliche, as is Vautrin's view of male friendship. The bond between men of genius is everything to Vautrin. His division of mankind into the weak and the strong, which is later to be echoed by Raskolnikov,[9] has its basis in this Romantic view of the male bond:

> You see, my lad, I live in a sphere raised above that of other men. . . . A man is everything to me, or nothing at all. He is less than nothing if he is a Poiret: you can crush him like a bug, he is flat and smelly. But a man is a god when he likes you; he is . . . a theatre where the finest sentiments find play, and I live only for sentiments. . . . Well, for me . . . only one real sentiment exists—friendship between man and man. (182–83)

The competitive hierarchy which makes society tick is in turn based upon this division between the ambitious strong men of the world and their contemptible underlings:

> Men give way before the power of genius, they hate it and try to blow upon it because it takes without sharing the plunder, but they give way if it persists; in short, they worship it on their knees when they have failed in their efforts to bury it under the mud. (129)

This competitive hierarchy is felt in relations with women as well:

> Ask women what kind of men they run after—'ambitious men' is the answer. The backs of the ambitious are stronger, their blood more rich in iron, their hearts warmer than those of other men. And a woman knows herself so happy and so lovely in the hours when she is strong, that she prefers above all men the man whose strength is enormous, even though it may mean her destruction. (126)

But Vautrin goes beyond Romanticism in his glorification of the male bond and the power hierarchy which results from it. Although he calls Rastignac a "god," he enjoys his own power over the young man. As in Dostoevsky's writings, this power of one man over another is sometimes symbolized in sexual terms, for Vautrin repeatedly compares Rastignac to a pretty, shy and virginal girl. His fascination with his own personal power over other human beings is reflected on another level in his ambition to become an American slave owner:

> I need two hundred thousand francs, for I want two hundred niggers to carry out my idea of the patriarchal life properly. Negroes, you see, are children ready-made that you can do what you like with, without a nosy public prosecutor coming to ask you questions about them. (131)

Both Balzac and Dostoevsky, then, begin their thoughts on power with the Romantic glorification of the man of genius, set apart from the rest of humanity, and with an interest in the bond between such special men. Both writers, however, go beyond this romantic beginning to a fascination with the dominance of one individual over another within that very bond. This leads to a preoccupation with power and dominance in social relationships and individual psychology, especially in Dostoevsky's works, where these power bonds are often exhibited at a more basic level.

The interest in bonding hierarchies in Russian (and world) literature did not begin with Dostoevsky, then. Neither did it end with him: there are passages in Tolstoy and Turgenev which are quite "Dostoevskian" in this regard.[10] But the theme of the competitive dominance hierarchy occupies a uniquely central position in the entire body of Dostoevsky's works and his treatment of the theme is distinctive.

him, or he may seek out those even lower than himself in that hierarchy and tyrannize over them. While most characters select one or the other of these alternatives, the underground man engages in both types of behavior, behaving masochistically with men who outrank him and sadistically with downtrodden women.

His experiences with an unnamed officer in Chapter 1 of Part 2 give us the best example of his masochistic attitude toward men above him in the hierarchy. Humorous in its bizarre way, this encounter begins as he sees someone being thrown out of a bar and muses that it would be pleasant to have a similar experience. He has a compulsion to reenact the experience of being forcibly and humiliatingly ejected from the company of his male peers, for the "mouse" passage quoted above, the rejection of the laws of nature and his experiences with Zverkov later in Part 2 follow this behavior paradigm. He enters the pub, and not only is he unable to engage anyone in a fight, he is absolutely ignored, particularly by one officer who moves him aside like a bug in order to get past. The underground man does not protest, although he later has a vivid fantasy about the humiliation he would endure if he did: "They would all simply split their sides with laughter, while the officer would not simply, that is inoffensively, beat me up a little, but would certainly kick me with his knee, bumping me thus around the billiard table, and then he might relent and let me out the window." (II 1) Instead he goes home and stews about it, behaving much like his "mouse," and during the next few years an extraordinary relationship develops between the two men, extraordinary partly because the officer never even knows about it. The underground man follows his officer, "Just as though tethered to him," monitors his actions on Nevsky Avenue, and finds out about him from janitors and the like. The underground man's feelings include the extremes of both hostility and affection:

> At last I made up my mind to challenge my opponent to a duel. I composed a beautiful and alluring letter to him, begging him to make his apologies to me; in case he refused I hinted quite definitely at a duel. The letter was written in such a way that if the officer understood even slightly 'the beautiful and lofty' he would certainly have run to me to throw himself on my neck and offer his friendship. And how fine that would have been! What a new life we could have begun! He could have defended me with his influence, while I could have benefitted him with my culture, and well, with ideas, and all sorts of things could have developed. (II 1)

The underground man's aggressive outpourings are mingled with friendly impulses. Because of his low self esteem, his perception of others is poisoned by envy, and as a result aggressive and friendly attitudes toward others are hopelessly confused. And again because of his self-hatred, this aggressive outreach is turned masochistically against himself. The confusion of aggression, affection and masochism is highlighted by the final lines of the chapter: "What's he doing now, my dear officer? Whom is he trampling?" (II 1)

The pages describing the actual duel are rich in literary allusion. Specifically, the passage parodies an incident in Chernyshevsky's *What Is To Be Done?* just as the whole book may be seen as a parody of that novel. But the more entertaining and interesting parallels, from our point of view, are with Gogol. The emphasis on Nevsky Avenue as the center of St. Petersburg society calls to mind Gogol's story bearing the name of that street, while the behavior of its pedestrians recalls the competitive masculine hierarchy characteristic of "The Nose" (see Chapter 2):

> I darted like a tiny fish, in a most disgusting manner, between the passers-by, always giving way either to generals, to cavalry or hussar officers, or to noblewomen. . . . [The officer] also stepped aside for generals and dignified personages and wiggled like a fish between them. But the likes of me, or even a cut above the likes of me, he simply trampled down. He would walk directly toward such people, as though there were only empty space in front of him, and under no circumstances would he step aside. I was drunk with spite, looking at him, and . . . spitefully stepped aside every time. It tormented me that even on the street I could not possibly be on an equal footing with him. (II 1)

Finally, he resolves to collide with his officer, not giving way and thus proving his equality. He takes great care that his clothing should be respectable for this pedestrian jousting match, in a passage that recalls Gogol's Akaky Akakievich and his excitement about his new overcoat. Finally the great day comes when the underground man's courage does not fail him and they collide. Even here one detects a trace of his perverse desire to be publicly beaten up by the officer, but he ignores the pain and declares that the "duel" has made them equals:

> Suddenly, three steps from my enemy I unexpectedly made up my mind, lowered my eyebrows and—we collided squarely, shoulder to shoulder. . . . Of course, I got the worst of it, since he was stronger, but that's not important. The point is, I achieved my goal, upheld my dignity, I didn't move aside one step, and I publicly placed myself on an equal social footing. (II 1)

Of course he does not really believe in this equality, but slinks off to his underground to lick his physical and psychological wounds.

We see something of the origin of these problems when the narrator describes his boyhood school experiences. His boarding school environment includes a typical adolescent pecking order. (II 3) It is a slightly younger version of the situation in Pushkin's "The Shot" (see chapter 2). At the top of the heap stands the young Zverkov, and the others fall happily into place.[10] But the "underground boy" has opted out of the group Zverkov leads. He hates Zverkov primarily because of that boy's supremacy, just as Pushkin's Silvio challenges a man to a duel for eclipsing his own social success. The underground boy does not have the money, rank, or good looks to compete in this masculine hierarchy, but he imbibes the spirit of the thing, coming to see relationships with other boys as fundamentally competitive.

First he challenges Zverkov openly. The pretext is Zverkov's braggadocio about his future affairs with women. This discussion has the character of a vicarious initiation to adulthood, especially since a formal initiation, the attainment of officer's epaulets, is mentioned as a prerequisite. At this crucial moment in group life and individual identity, the underground boy refuses to accept his subordinate role and attacks Zverkov for his vulgarity and inhumanity. Thus his first response to the overwhelming rival and model is to deny his own desire for the sexual object which binds the boys together. In Girard's terms, he denies the fact of mediated desire.

His next response is the solipsistic one: "I hated them from the first and shut myself away from them in defensive, wounded and excessive pride. . . . I began to consider them beneath me. . . .I constantly thirsted for their humiliation." (II 3) Finally he tries to set up a competing hierarchy, echoing Pechorin's views on friendship: "I once had a friend. But I was already a despot at heart; I wanted unlimited power over his soul. . . . He was a naive and submissive soul, but when he surrendered to me completely, I immediately conceived a hatred for him and repulsed him. It was as though I needed him only for the sake of my triumph over him, only for his submission." (II 3) The underground man exhibits these very behavior patterns as an adult. In a sense he is frozen in adolescence. He calls himself a "boy" (*malchishka,* II 1).

When the underground man plans to crash his friends' little class reunion it is with mingled ideas of friendship and aggression: "I dreamed of gaining the upper hand, of conquering them, of captivating them and making them like me. . . . They would desert Zverkov, he would sit in a corner, silent and ashamed, and I would crush him." (II 3) He links friendship with aggression to the end; he can conceive of no way of gaining friendship except by force. He must "compel them to like him" and by doing so he will "crush Zverkov": "Either they will all implore my friendship on their knees, embracing my feet, or . . . or I will slap Zverkov." (II 4) But it is himself that he annihilates, placing himself in exactly the position in which he wished to see Zverkov: "Everyone deserted me, and I sat crushed and annihilated." (II 4) A true masochist, he constructs the situation so that he himself will be placed in the position in which he wished to see his enemy, and the aggression he directs against his enemy will fall upon his own head. True to solipsistic form he denies the existence of his persecutors: "I think of you as pawns, as nonexistent pawns." (II 4) He is compelled to reenact the drama of his rejection and humiliation by his male peers, ostensibly staged as an attempt to compel them to accept him into their circle. This results in his denial of their existence, ironically reflecting the fact that he himself has been "reduced to nothing." (*u–nichto–zhen,* 'an–nihil–ated').

The underground man is a parody of Silvio,[11] and the worst of it is that he knows this. Observe his fantasy as he chases after his friends on the way to the brothel:

> In 15 years I will seek him out in some provincial town. He will be married and happy. . . . I will say: 'Look, monster, look at my sunken cheeks and my rags! I've lost everything—career, happiness, art, science, *the woman I loved,* and all because of you. Here are pistols. I came to discharge my pistol and . . . and I forgive you.' At that point I will fire into the air and disappear without a trace . . . I almost began to cry, even though I knew perfectly well that at that very moment that it was all out of Silvio. . . . (II 5)

The ability to see that he is a literary parody, without being able to alter that fact, intensifies the underground man's agony of self-consciousness. This very trait of self analysis is inherited from Pechorin and other late Romantic heroes. Like Pechorin, the underground man is divided into actor and observer. So both in his attitude toward himself and in his relations with others, the underground man is Silvio and Pechorin turned inside-out, with the veil which made them seem romantic pulled embarrassingly aside.

With socially inferior men the underground man engages in the same sort of unsuccessful struggle for personal dominance, but here his masochistic behavior produces an inversion of the social hierarchy. His servant, Apollon, behaves as his master:

> He was my plague, a scourge sent to me by providence. We had bickered constantly for several years running, and I hated him. . . . He treated me quite despotically, spoke to me very seldom, and if he happened to glance at me, then he would look with a hard, majestically self-assured and

constantly mocking look, which sometimes drove me wild. . . . There could be no doubt that he considered me the greatest fool on earth, and if he 'kept me on,' it was only so that he might receive his salary every month. (II 8)

The qualities he attributes to Apollon, self-confidence, despotism, and mocking contempt for others, are the very ones he would like to possess himself, and the fact that he retains the servant shows that he finds Apollon's real or imagined despotism somehow appealing.

In his relations with other men, then, the underground man is so convinced of his low position in the competitive sexual hierarchy that he revels in humiliation and "nothingness." In his relations with women, on the other hand, the sadistic side of his personality is revealed.

At the height of his own humiliation he chases Zverkov and friends to the brothel where they have decided to continue their revels. Back in school he had challenged Zverkov over sexual issues; now he implicitly accepts Zverkov's dominance by following him to the brothel. There he meets Liza, who, as a woman, and a prostitute at that, is a being even lower than himself in the hierarchy of sexual identity and human worth. As he behaves masochistically with those above him in this hierarchy, so he treats those beneath him sadistically. He delights in the power he holds over Liza and he toys with her emotions, arousing her hope and despair by turns. First he paints a grim picture of her position in the brothel, placing particular emphasis on her bondage, and contrasting her with himself:

> Although I may cover myself with filth, yet I am no one's slave. I come and go as I please. I shake it all off and am a new man. But you must admit that you are a slave from the very start. Yes, a slave! You give up everything, your entire will. And later you'll want to tear off these chains, but you can't. Stronger and stronger they will bind you. (II 6)

Then he raises her hopes by painting a vivid picture of the joys of family life. A moment later, angered by her reply, he returns to a shattering vision of her eventual death in the brothel. He is fascinated by his ability to gain power over her:

> I had long foreseen by this time that I had turned her head completely and shattered her spirit, and the more convinced I became of it, the more anxious I became to achieve my goal as quickly and completely as possible. The game, the game appealed to me. (II 7)

This exercise in personal domination has a sexual component, for her responses seem almost orgasmic:

> She lay face down, her face pressed firmly into the pillow which she was grasping with both hands. Her breast was bursting. Her whole young

> body shook, as though in convulsions. . . . She bit the pillow, she bit her
> hand until blood came . . . and grew rigid with effort, holding her breath
> and clenching her teeth. (II 7)

After this she is submissive with the underground man and gazes at him as
"children look at those they love very much and from whom they are
requesting something." (II 7) The connection between children and sexually
oppressed women is a recurring theme in Dostoevsky's works.

After this encounter the underground man indulges in a romantic fantasy about the life he might have with Liza, treating himself to the same
sort of glowing picture he had painted for her in his rhapsody on family
life:

> I, for instance, save Liza. . . . I develop her, educate her. At last I notice
> that she loves me. . . . At last she . . . throws herself at my feet and
> declares that I am her savior. . . . 'Liza,' I say, ' do you think I have not
> noticed your love? I saw everything, . . . but I haven't wanted to be the
> first to encroach upon your heart, since I had influence over you, and
> that . . . is despotism. . . . But now, now—you are mine, you are my
> creation. . . .
>
> And into my house boldly and freely
> Enter as complete mistress!' (II 8)

Note that the fantasy revolves around the idea of personal domination.
First he congratulates himself for restraining his will to power, then exults
that she belongs to him, and finally reverses this by quoting poetry declar-
ing that she commands him.

What a different picture we get when she actually arrives! She discovers
him in a humiliating position: he is wearing a shabby dressing gown, his
poor apartment is a mess, and he is getting the worst of an argument with
Apollon. His position in the power hierarchy has been reversed, and he
swears revenge upon her for his humiliation. Finally, he describes for her
the background of his earlier behavior in the brothel: "I had been humiliated, so I wanted to humiliate; they had turned me into a rag, so I wanted
to show my power." (II 9) She responds by falling back, "as though she had
been struck with an axe" (II 9, the image is doubly significant for readers familiar with *Crime and Punishment*). She responds sympathetically to
his hysterics and he is finally reduced to a position identical to hers in the
brothel: "And at this point . . . lying face down on the sofa, rigidly, with
my face thrust into my tattered leather cushion . . . it occurred to me that
our roles had indeed been decisively reversed." (II 9) But a new reversal
takes place immediately and they have another sadomasochistic sexual
encounter:

In my heart suddenly another feeling was ignited and flared up . . . a feeling of mastery and possession. My eyes glittered with passion and I squeezed her hand hard. How I hated her and how I was attracted to her at that moment. One feeling intensified the other. It was almost like revenge! . . . She rapturously and hotly embraced me. (II 9)

Through all of this the underground man, with his diseased self-awareness, is fully cognizant of each role reversal and of the fascination with power which motivates his behavior. Finally he explains it thus:

I could not even love, for I repeat, to love for me meant to tyrannize and morally dominate. All my life I have not been able even to imagine any other kind of love and I have now come to the point of thinking sometimes that love consists in the right, willfully given by the love object, to tyrannize over him. Even in my underground dreams I have not conceived of love otherwise than as a battle. I have always begun it with hatred and ended with moral domination, and then I could never imagine what to do with the vanquished object. (II 10)

All human relationships are based on power for the underground man. In romantic relationships he takes voluptuous delight in exercising his power over others, while in relationships with other men he enjoys the power that others exercise over him. This is perhaps the fundamental problem in human relationships as far as Dostoevsky is concerned. One might say that it constitues his concept of original sin. *Notes from Underground* is the grimmest of his works, the *Inferno* of his *Divine Comedy*,[12] and here he presents no solution to these problems. This work initiates the mature period of his creative life, and the great novels that follow *Notes from Underground* may be seen as attempts to work out the fundamental problems of personal dominance presented here.

Not all of Dostoevsky's depictions of hierarchical behavior are as morbid as *Notes from Underground,* however. His humorous pieces revolve around the same issues. In "Small Sketches," a journalistic sketch published in an 1872 miscellany, he describes the jockeying for status among the aristocrats on a pleasure cruise. Two highly placed authorities, a provincial administrator and a retired court figure, want to strike up a conversation, but cannot resolve questions of rank between them in order to do so. They are assisted by a grovelling "second class" gentleman who is only too happy to take a subservient role in order to bring his betters together. This man is content with his status, and will never try to change it. Just as in Dostoevsky's earliest sketches, such men are seen as indispensable to society. A "Europeanized" gentleman wishes to increase his status by joining the conversation, and is under considerable pressure from his socially climbing wife to do so, but he cannot find an opening:

> He is even about to stroke the [dignitary's] setter so as to start in some-how, but he disdainfully draws back his already outstretched hand and suddenly even feels an irresistible urge to give the setter a kick with his foot. Gradually he assumes a somewhat withdrawn and offended expres-sion and walks away for a moment. . . .

He hates the "second class" gentleman with all his heart. Finally he makes a disastrous and ludicrous attempt to join the conversation and is covered with ignominy. The social hierarchy is here reduced to farce, but the com-ponents are the same as those of *Notes from Underground*: status, aggressive/ submissive ambivalence and withdrawal into the self. Similar passages in *The Diary of a Writer* outline the combination of imposing demeanor and the urge to defer to superiors in the typical Russian gentleman.

Two short novels written soon after the return from Siberia, *Uncle's Dream* and *The Village of Stepanchikovo* (*The Friend of the Family*), deal humorously with power struggles in provincial society. The hero of the latter novel is Foma Fomich, a vain nonentity who exercises complete tyranny over a provincial family. He does this, ironically, by claiming to be dominated and brutally treated by them. He has been in a subservient posi-tion during most of his life, and this produces his peculiar technique of control through apparent subservience. "A base soul escaping from oppres-sion loves to oppress others. Foma had been oppressed, and at the same time he felt a craving to oppress others." (13) The work is thus based on an inversion of the apparent power structure in which real power is achieved through alleged submission. Foma Fomich is finally overthrown, but his misfortunes after being kicked out cause the family to reinstate him out of pity. The plot structure is based on multiple inversions of the power bal-ance. Such inversions are often pivotal in Dostoevsky's works, usually with serious moral implications. Here the same paradigm is the object of humorous treatment.

Dostoevsky's own biography provides several examples of behavior and relationships similar to those found in *Notes from Underground*. It is easy to see why he was drawn to literary accounts of such phenomena. His rela-tionship with his fellow writer Ivan Turgenev is a case in point. Shortly before Dostoevsky's death, he described Turgenev to a young friend as a man who always had to have preeminence in everything.[13] This is certainly how he is depicted in *The Devils*, where the portrayal of the pompous writer Karmazinov satirizes Turgenev's vanity and European ways. The two writ-ers became friends as young men in Belinsky's literary circle in St. Peters-burg during the late 1840's. Dostoevsky had just received phenomenal acclaim for his first novel, *Poor Folk*, and the success had gone to his head.

His vanity was incommensurate with his achievements, and yet memoirist Avdotya Panaeva noted that his arrogance was obviously the product of shyness and nervous insecurity. Indeed, he felt overwhelmed by the urbane and aristocratic young *literati* who formed his new circle of friends, in particular the well-educated and polished Turgenev. Not having a particularly distinguished background himself, Dostoevsky was ill at ease in high society. At first he was quite taken with Turgenev's friendly advances toward him, was even "in love" with Turgenev as only a young Romantic could be. But Turgenev and his friends soon tired of the young Dostoevsky's hauteur and finally lampooned him both in a journal and in public. Dostoevsky was crushed, and his relations with Turgenev were strained at best for the rest of his life.[14]

These incidents fit the pattern observed above in *Notes from Underground*. Turgenev was admired as a paragon of every perfection toward which Dostoevsky might have aspired. He was welcomed as a friend, but he was also feared as a threat to Dostoevsky's own security. By an attitude of overweening pride Dostoevsky brought about the rejection he feared from his admired competitor, and thus destroyed his own fragile sense of security.

Within several frames of reference, psychopathological, humorous, and also biographical, we can see how a preoccupation with hierarchical bonding was central to Dostoevsky's literary career. The figure of the emotional solipsist, with his alternating aggressive and submissive behavior, is a crucially important figure in his novels. Fearing rejection from others, he produces that rejection, and then tries to mask it by rejecting others in turn. This behavior produces a web of sadistic and masochistic relationships in a dominance hierarchy. The inversion of that power hierarchy is the central behavioral paradigm in Dostoevsky's fictional world. Ultimately such inversions become the crucial redemptive act in his moral world as well.

CHAPTER 4

IDENTITY CRISIS AND CHARACTER DOUBLING

Dostoevsky's underground man has trouble defining himself in relation to others. His fuzzy concept of his own identity produces his exaggerated and contradictory reactions to others, his worship of the officer, his hatred of Zverkov, his resentment of Apollon, and his cruelty to Liza. Mikhail Bakhtin has noted that the structural center of a Dostoevskian work is the hero's concept of himself.[1] This is nowhere truer than in *Notes from Underground*, where the most important tensions arise from the very fact that the hero never resolves the questions of his own identity which so torment him. In each of his encounters with others he attempts to test his ego, to see himself anew through the eyes of others.[2] It is significant that the hero is one of the only characters in the work whose name we are not told. The underground man does not know who he is.

One of the functions of the dominance hierarchy is to give each member of society a sense of identity. When each individual is satisfied with his status, no matter how low, the group remains stable.[3] Makar Devushkin, the low-ranking copy clerk of Dostoevsky's first novel, *Poor Folk,* accepts his own low status and even warmly defends the hierarchy as a useful principle of social organization (July 8). As a result, the pathos of that novel is static and sentimental rather than tragic. The drama in Dostoevsky's novels begins when a character uncertain of his position in the hierarchy begins to experiment with identity or status. Raskolnikov's murder in *Crime and Punishment* is an example of such an existential experiment. Raskolnikov is going through a self-administered initiation rite, trying to determine whether he belongs to the special class of men who stand at the top of the hierarchy (represented by Napoleon) or to the lowest category (the louse, a term he even uses to describe the woman he murders).

The difficulty such a character has in drawing the boundary line between self and other is symptomatic of his inability to define himself. Unable to accept or understand his own identity, he perceives others as invincible forces threatening to engulf him. As we have seen in the last chapter, his immediate reaction is the defensive one of denying the reality of the world outside himself. This solipsistic device, ironically, demonstrates his fears of his own unreality. Ultimately, he does not know where the world ends and the self begins.

In *Civilization and Its Discontents,* Freud described the separation of the ego from the object world in infancy. First the object world is included in the primary ego. All the world is interpreted as an extension of the self. Then gradually the idea of the non-self makes its appearance and the ego is separated from the world.[5] For Dostoevsky's pathological characters this process becomes a threat to the self as the non-self becomes larger and more powerful and threatens to engulf the insecure self.

Vyacheslav Ivanov maintained that Dostoevsky's characters have the laudable ability to encounter another ego as subject rather than as object. There is truth in this observation, but the ability has both a positive and a negative aspect, as Ivanov himself admitted. Characters like the underground man identify so thoroughly with the non-self as subject that the self becomes object for them. For these characters the process of ego separation described by Freud is distorted and the individual sides with the non-self rather than with the ego. They view themselves from a vantage point attributed to others, and continually struggle to define themselves in the uncomplimentary light. This strong identification of the self with the non-self results in the inability to distinguish the two and finally in the refusal to accept the reality of a genuine non-self. For Ivanov (as for Father Zosima in *The Brothers Karamazov*) this problem was solved by religious faith, but he admitted that otherwise it resulted in solipsistic nihilism.[5]

Since the confusion of self and other results from a profound devaluation of the self, it produces a deification of the other. As René Girard puts it, men become gods to one another. Sadism and masochism, the sacraments of this underground religion, turn out to be fundamentally the same phenomenon.[6] In a world where self and other are hopelessly confused, any attitude toward the non-self may be rapidly converted into an attitude toward the self.[7]

In Dostoevsky's works this convoluted process is symbolized by the technique of character doubling. Many of Dostoevsky's characters encounter other beings who represent themselves in the world outside. Some critics have seen this phenomenon as a central structural principle in Dostoevsky's novels.[8] His second novel, for which he always entertained great hopes, is even entitled *The Double.* Characters like Raskolnikov and Stavrogin in the major novels are surrounded by minor characters who double them in various ways.

Unfortunately, previous discussions of this phenomenon have been marred by vagueness, since the term has been used to describe several different, yet related, phenomena. The concept becomes clearer if we make certain basic distinctions. First we may distinguish between internal and external doubling, that is, the division may be within the character himself, or he may encounter his alter ego in the world outside himself. More refinement is possible: internal doubling may be psychological or supernatural (it is usually both to some extent) while external doubling may be parallel (Raskolnikov and Svidrigailov, Stavrogin and Kirillov) or contrastive (Myshkin and Rogozhin, Velchaninov and Trusotsky). External doubling will be taken up in Chapter 5. The present chapter will deal with internal doubling.

Almost all of Dostoevsky's major characters are characterized by internal psychological doubling. We have observed, for instance, the opposition of sadistic and masochistic impulses in the underground man. Raskolnikov's very name suggests a similar internal division (from *raskol* 'split,' 'schism'). Versilov in *A Raw Youth* is divided into two contrasting selves (III 10 II, III 13 I). In this regard all of these characters are descendants of Lermontov's Pechorin, with his division into actor and observer. Girard speaks of the division of the self into a "contemptible being" and a "contemptuous observer." This observer is the other within the self, and external doubling takes place when this internal double is personified by a being in the outside world.[9]

On the boundary between internal and external doubling, Dostoevsky uses the Gothic device of the supernatural double to express a disturbed character's attitudes toward self and other. The device is a commonplace one, used in works like Poe's "William Wilson," Stevenson's *Dr. Jekyll and Mr. Hyde* and Wilde's *The Picture of Dorian Gray,* to suggest a division between good and evil selves.[10] All of these writers use the double to depict a moral division within their troubled heroes. Each of these men has a good self and a bad self. In Dostoevsky's hands the device is a more complex tool for portraying a psychological, rather than a moral, division within the self. Ivan Karamazov's devil is such a supernatural double, but Dostoevsky first used the device in his second novel, *The Double.* Dostoevsky himself admitted that this work is flawed in execution. Its reception by the public fell short of the author's high hopes. The work is derivative, relying heavily on Gogol's "Diary of a Madman" and "The Nose." Yet Dostoevsky correctly maintained throughout his career that the idea of the work had great promise. In fact the ideas expressed in *The Double* are crucial to an understanding of Dostoevskian psychology.

Yakov Petrovich Golyadkin, the hero of *The Double,* is a creature poised on the edge of non-being, and in the encounter with himself as other he expresses complex attitudes toward the world and the self. His name suggests nakedness (*golyj* 'naked'), and in the Russian tradition this signifies poverty rather than anything sexual. It also may suggest a sense of social inadequacy, a problem from which Yakov Petrovich suffers chronically. On the morning in question he rises from his bed and immediately looks in the mirror, as though to reaffirm the reality of his existence. It soon becomes clear that this is a very special day for Yakov Petrovich. He has saved money to rent carriage and livery for the day and plans to ride about in style. (These details echo those of Gogol's stories "The Nose" and "The Overcoat." In the first, the hero rises and looks in the mirror to examine a pimple, only to discover with horror that his nose is missing. In the second, the protagonist makes elaborate preparations for donning his new over-coat. Dostoevsky echoes the latter detail again in *Notes from Underground* where the protagonist makes similar preparations for his meeting with the lieutenant.) As he rides about, however, he is embarrassed to meet his acquaintances, and tries to efface himself: "He fearfully squeezed himself into the darkest corner of the carriage." (I) A moment later he questions himself: "Shall I acknowledge them or not? . . . or shall I pretend that it's not me, but someone else, strikingly similar to me, and look as though nothing had happened. Just as though it's not me, not me, and that's all there is to it! . . ." Finally he speaks to his acquaintance: "I, I'm all right (*ya nichego*), . . . I'm perfectly all right. It's not me at all, Andrei Filippo-vich, not me at all. . . ." (I) Unfortunately it isnot possible to convey in English the suggestion conveyed by the colloquial Russian expresssion "*Ya nichego!*" translated here as "I'm all right." Understood literally, it could be interpreted to mean, "I am nothing." (*Ya nichto* would be technically more correct, but *Ya nichego* suggests the same possibility.) This parallels Makar Devushkin's persistent assertions of his own nothingness in *Poor Folk*.

Golyadkin is particularly affected by the penetrating gaze of others, and even of inanimate objects:

> Mr. Golyadkin perceived a desire to sink through the ground or hide, together with his carriage, in a mouse-hole. It seems to him that every-thing whatever in Olsufy Ivanovich's house was now staring at him from all the windows. He knew that if he turned round he would certainly die on the spot. (III)

He tries to bolster his flagging identity by looking in mirrors whenever the opportunity arises, and by destroying others with:

> the same challenging stare which possessed the exceptional power to reduce to ashes all the enemies of Mr. Golyadkin. Furthermore, this stare fully expressed Mr. Golyadkin's independence, that is, it stated clearly that Mr. Golyadkin was perfectly all right (*nichego*), that he was all on his own, like everyone else. . . . (I)

He visited his doctor and tells him, "I go my own way, . . . my own particu-lar way. . . . I am a man apart, and, as far as I can see, I don't depend on anybody." (II) He protests too much; it is clear that he is trying to convince himself. His ontological insecurity becomes even clearer when the doctor asks him where he used to live. He misunderstands him and replies "I was living, Christian Ovanovich, I was living even formerly. How could it be otherwise?" (II)

Finally he crashes a party at his boss's mansion and finds himself totally out of place. This expedition has an amatory basis, for he carries a torch for his boss's daughter, but he is utterly incapable of expressing his romantic feeling. He feels insignificant in the presence of other guests, particularly "an officer, a tall and handsome young man before whom Mr. Golyadkin felt an utter insect," (IV), and he repeatedly tries to efface himself under their "annihilating stares." He also tries to bring them down to his level. He observes that one "very respectable looking gentleman . . . is wearing a wig, . . . and if that wig were removed he would have a naked head, just like my naked palm." (IV) By imaginatively undressing the other guests he brings upon them a humiliation not unlike that suggested by his own name and his current embarrassing situation. This comforts him, and soon his fantasies become even more aggressive. He imagines that the chandelier falls on the guests, obliging him to rescue his sweetheart. The chandelier does not fall, however. Instead, Mr. Golyadkin is thrown out and feels himself "falling into an abyss." (V)

At this point we are told that he was "slain—utterly slain, in the full sense of the word." (I 138)

> . . .Mr. Golyadkin looked as though he were trying to hide somewhere away from himself. Yes, it really was so! We will say more: Mr. Golyadkin wanted not only to run away from himself at that moment, but even to annihilate himself, to cease to be, to return to the dust. . . . in that moment he died and disappeared. . . ." (V)

It is at this point that he encounters his double, a person exactly like himself in every respect. In other words, just when his worst ontological fears of personal non-existence are realized, he encounters himself as other.[11]

The second Mr. Golyadkin, although physically like the hero in every respect, has all of the characteristics that the hero lacks and longs to have. He is socially adept and soon becomes intimate with all the highly placed personages our hero would like to impress. He is a model of what Mr. Golyadkin would like to be, and his presence occasions all of the feelings of envy, resentment and love which Girard discusses with reference to "mimetic desire." He comes to work at the same office and rapidly moves up the ladder of success.

He was Mr. Golyadkin himself—not the Mr. Golyadkin . . . who liked to stay in the background and bury himself in the crowd—no, this was another Mr. Golyadkin, a completely different one, but at the same time quite similar to the other . . . (VI)

The rightful Mr. Golyadkin, convinced at first that this is a plot instigated by his "enemies," is outraged and offended. But there is a strong note of envy in his attitude toward the upstart: "He looks like the favorite, that scoundrel! I'd like to know how he gets on so in high society. . . . I'd like to find out just what it is he whispers to all of them." (X) His fascination with the double looks for awhile as though it may turn into friendship, and the two Golyadkins get drunk together. The real one says,

"Well, you and I Yakov Petrovich, we'll get on together. (*soidyomsya,* lit. 'come together,' 'merge'). . . . you and I, Yakov Petrovich, we'll live like fish in water, like real brothers; we'll be clever, buddy, we'll outwit them together (*zaodno,* lit. 'as one'), we'll be the ones to intrigue against them." (VIII)

This feeling of collusion bolsters his ego considerably: ". . . not only did he not fear his enemies, but he was even ready now to challenge all of them to decisive combat. . . . He had become a patron and protector in his own right. . . ." (VI) All of this is occasioned by his pity for his double's temporary (and feigned) poverty and meekness. As long as he can maintain a superior position with regard to his friend he does not feel threatened.

In fact, the attitudes and behavior of the characters change radically, abruptly and frequently in the last two-thirds of the work. After the appearance of the double it becomes clear that the logic of the work is dream logic. The line between reality and fantasy is purposely left indistinct, just as is the line between self and others. We never even know for certain whether the double is real or imaginary.[12] This dreamlike shifting of emotional stance reflects the complex and contradictory nature of Golyadkin's feelings toward himself and others. Feelings toward the world outside and feelings toward the self are frequently confused in Dostoevsky's work, particularly if they are hostile feelings. But nowhere else is this identity of inward and outward directed feelings so explicit as here, using the device of the double which is at once both self and other. In terms of professional and social success, the double is a successful version of Golyadkin himself; the unsuccessful clerk may experience success vicariously through his alter ego. In the drinking scene this is represented by its opposite, and the double becomes a weak individual to be protected, just as Golyadkin himself feels a need to be protected by a successful counterpart. The device of the double allows two contradictory attitudes toward the self and others to be expressed at once.

Likewise his antagonistic feelings toward the second Golyadkin suggest self-directed hostility. The hostility is directed outward and inward at once, as in this passage: "[The Double] was such an unsavory character, his habits were so mischievous, so base; he was such a scoundrel, such a frivolous sycophantic lickspittle, such a Golyadkin!" The usurper's attitude toward the rightful Goyadkin is equally contemptuous:

> Mr. Golyadkin . . . triumphantly clasped the hand of the man he had called his deadly enemy. But what was his astonishment, frenzy and rage . . . when his enemy and mortal foe, the ignoble Mr. Golyadkin junior . . . suddenly with intolerable impudence and rudeness tore his hand from the hand of Mr. Golyadkin senior. Not only that, he shook off his hand as though he had soiled it with something altogether unpleasant. Not only that, he spat to the side accompanying all this with the most offensive gesture. Not only that, he took out his handkerchief and, right there, in the most outrageous fashion, wiped it with his fingers which had been for a moment in the hand of Mr. Golyadkin senior. (X)

This deliberate public humiliation by an identical double is a powerful symbol of revulsion against the self.[13]

At one point this self-directed hostility is symbolized in a way which is clearly masochistic, symbolically suggesting the idea of self-castration:

> "Well, if some sort of magician should appear now, or if somehow or other they would say officially, 'Give up a finger of your right hand, Golyadkin, and you are quits. There will be no other Golyadkin and you will be happy, only without your finger—I would give up the finger, I would certainly give it up, without blinking I would give it up."

The sexual meaning is not the only one possible here. In Dostoevsky's late novels there is much biting of fingers, in which the image has a more generalized meaning. Kirillov bites Pyotr Verkhovensky's finger in *The Devils* (imitating Stavrogin who has bitten the governor's ear), Ilyusha Snegiryov bites Alyosha's finger in *The Brothers Karamazov*, and Liza Khokhlakova, imitating Alyosha's injury, smashes her finger in a door. In the context of *The Double*, however, given its preoccupation with issues of personal identity, the idea of castration suggests itself as the strongest possibility for the meaning of this image. Earlier in the same passage, Golyadkin had exclaimed, "There it is, then, I'll overcome by submitting. Where's the danger in that?" (XI) Likewise in the closing sentences of the works, as Golyadkin is being carted off to the asylum, he tries, "trembling with timidity, . . . to mollify the terrible doctor with submissiveness and humility." His words to the doctor are "I'm all right" (*Ya nichego*, lit. "I am nothing.") So for all his aggressive raging against his persecutors, the masochistic alternative is finally more amenable to the unfortunate Mr. Golyadkin.

Just as in *Notes from Underground*, where the contrasting relations with superiors and inferiors in the power hierarchy demonstrated the protagonist's conflicting feelings, here the device of the doubled self makes manifest Golyadkin's deep ambivalence toward himself and toward the world outside. The encounter with the self as other is the ultimate ontological crisis for the insecure Dostoevskian psychopath, and in this encounter he treats the other with aggression and self-effacement by turns, while in the person of his alter ego he showers upon himself both the acceptance he desires and the contempt he fears.

CHAPTER 5

THE FRIEND AS ENEMY

Doubling takes place in Dostoevsky's works when the dual attitude toward the self becomes so strongly bifurcated that the character in question seems to have two opposing personalities. In *The Double,* the second personality begins to become external, at least in the hero's deranged fantasy if not, as alleged, in fact. In later works, the double often becomes external through the agency of another character who responds to the protagonist in an extraordinary way. The character is "splintered," to use A. L. Bem's term (*droblenie lichnosti*), and various qualities are projected onto other characters who either echo those qualities or represent the opposite qualities.[1] Sometimes the double is a parallel figure, echoing some special aspect of the hero's character, often an aspect which is hidden from public view. Elsewhere the double is the hero's opposite, just as Golyadkin's double has all the traits he himself lacks. Such contrastive doubling binds the characters in an explosive combination of self-denying love and competitive hatred.[2]

Contrastive doubling is exemplified by *The Idiot,* which opens with, and to some extent revolves around, the contrast between Myshkin and Rogozhin. The differences between the two are extreme, so the relationship between them becomes one of complementation. Their unity depends on the contrast, or even opposition, between them. For this very reason the friendship is intense, and for this very reason it borders on hatred. In fact the relationship between Myshkin and Rogozhin is a more mature treatment of the issues dealt with in *The Double.*[3]

The contrast proceeds along lines suggested in the previous chapter. The emotionally isolated Dostoevskian psychopath can deal with the world either aggressively or passively, and these two characters dramatize the alternatives. Rogozhin is the aggressive one. He is physically strong, although his pallor gives him an "emaciated" look, and he approaches the world with a contemptuous sneer. In the first quarter of the novel he storms about with a band of followers that reminds one of a princely retinue, and when he comes on stage the plot crackles with activity.[4] Yet one of the peculiar things about his presence in the novel is the infrequency of his actual appearances. He is certainly one of the major characters of the book, but his power is felt more in his absence than in his presence. Myshkin is constantly aware of Rogozhin's burning eyes upon him in an anonymous crowd, but Rogozhin appears rarely. Of course this is a novelist's trick, fashioned from a series of Romantic and Gothic literary devices, to keep the reader fascinated with this enigmatic character. His physical portrait relies on cliches of Byronic heroism, he is kept out of sight save at dramatic moments, and we are reminded from time to time of his burning eyes staring at Myshkin out of the crowd.[5] But the trick works; an aura of mysterious and slightly hideous animal power surrounds Rogozhin throughout the novel.

Myshkin, with his fair hair and almost white beard and dreamy eyes, is absolutely spiritual and Christlike, and it is precisely the kenotic or passive elements of Christ that are stressed in his character.[6] His meekness, naivete and humility draw people to him and at the same time set him apart from the rest of humanity. It is these qualities as much as his epilepsy which make people assume he is mentally deficient as well as sexually impotent. The connection between epilepsy and asexuality is a curious fiction, brought into the novel to reinforce this idea of Myshkin as a being set apart by his half-insane purity, but in which Dostoevsky, himself a sexually active epileptic, surely did not believe. When Nastasya Filippovna first meets Myshkin, she takes him for a servant since he opens the door for her at the Ivolgins' apartment, and he, making no attempt to correct her, picks up her coat and announces her. He assumes the role of servant, and he is continually taking upon himself the suffering of others. In the scene immediately following his announcement of Nastasya Filippovna, he steps between Ganya Ivolgin and his sister Varya to take the slap Ganya intends for Varya. Myshkin stands for Christ as suffering servant, continually placing himself below others, absorbing the abuse of others, and returning forgiveness in exchange for it.

The most extended encounter between Myshkin and Rogozhin occurs in Part 2 of the novel in Rogozhin's house, a structure pervaded by a stolid and gloomy physicality which reinforces the characterization of Rogozhin. A painting by Holbein hangs over the doorway, a painting of Christ in the tomb, remarkable for its ruthlessly realistic portrayal of the ugly physicality and mortality of the corpse. Several characters describe this painting in the course of the novel, remarking that it might cause one to lose one's faith. Rogozhin's physical and dead Christ wars with Myshkin's spiritual one.

The house is tenanted by a family of Skoptsy, members of a sect notable for its rigid power structure and particularly for its practice of mortification of the flesh through self-castration. One might expect this detail to be associated with Myshkin, reinforcing his self-abnegating spirituality. Its mention in connection with Rogozhin suggests that sexual self-mutilation is a possible alternative for him. Indeed, Rogozhin's sexual escapades do turn out to be self-destructive as well as destructive of others.

The friendship between the two men becomes much closer in this encounter. They begin to use the familiar pronoun with each other and they pledge their brotherhood by exchanging crosses. The cross symbolizes Myskin's spirituality and it reinforces the bond of friendship between them just as the other physical object which is important in this encounter, the knife, symbolizes Rogozhin's sexuality and it comes to represent the hostile aspects of their relationship.[7] This is the very knife with which Rogozhin will later kill Nastasya Filippovna. Its sexual overtones are unmistakable. As the two friends are talking Myshkin twice picks up the knife and handles it absentmindedly. Both times Rogozhin takes it from him angrily. They devote an inordinate amount of attention to it and Rogozhin's feelings about it are intense:

> It was a fairly simple sort of knife with no sheath, with a horn handle, a seven inch blade and a corresponding breadth.
> Seeing that Myshkin had taken special notice of the fact that the knife had been twice taken out of his hands, Rogozhin grabbed it in angry irritation, put it in the book, and tossed the book on another table.
> "Do you cut pages with it or something?"
> "Yes, I do."
> "But it's a garden knife?"
> "Yes, it is, Can't one cut pages with a garden knife?"
> "But it's . . . brand new."
> "What if it is? Why can't I buy a new knife?" Rogozhin cried in a frenzy at last, growing more irritated at every word. (II 3)

The chapter which follows this encounter is quite strange, even irritating in its vagueness and confusion. Myshkin wanders around St. Petersburg in the early evening hours, musing absentmindedly. This seems to be typical of his mental activity before a seizure. He jumps from one thought to another with no apparent motivation, and the narrator is exasperatingly imprecise about the content of his thoughts. The connections between ideas and the lack of clarity of those ideas are quite dreamlike.[8] Rogozhin seems to be following him, or at least Myshkin senses the presence of his friend's burning eyes. One of the thoughts which recurs, and which he connects with Rogozhin, is the memory of a knife which he saw in a shop window that morning. At first the narrator resolutely refuses to tell us that the object in question is a knife, suggesting that Myshkin is repressing its identity for some reason. The possibility of repression is reinforced by the feeling of loathing which Myshkin experiences at each new reference to the object, which is called simply "item for sale" (*tovar*) using the unusual singular form. Myshkin finds the store once again and values the object at sixty kopeks. "It's certainly not worth more," he says with a laugh. The second time he thinks of the "item" it is still not named, but we are told that it was in the window of a cutlery dealer, making its identity clear.

The knife represents the possibility of Rogozhin's murderous attack on Nastasya Filippovna, perhaps upon Myshkin himself, and each thought of the knife occasions in Myshkin feelings of shame. On one level he is simply reproaching himself for doing nothing to avert the murder. But on another level the object which symbolizes his friend's difference from himself, with clear sexual overtones, brings about a feeling of personal inadequacy. He even accuses himself of "womanliness." This is followed in Constance Garnett's translation by a passage left out of recent Soviet editions, in which Myshkin finally makes the connection between the knife in the shop window and the one on Rogozhin's table. Immediately after this: "A new, unbearable surge of shame, almost of despair, rooted him to the spot . . . 'Yes, I am a man of no heart and a coward.'" (II 4) On one level this sort of self-deprecation reminds us of Golyadkin's or the underground man's insecurities or of Raskolnikov's desire to prove that he is a man and not "a louse." But the sudden intensity of the reaction and its clear link to Rogozhin's knife makes it evident that Myshkin is responding to his alter ego here, and specifically to his qualities of aggressiveness and sexuality. The issues of personal identification binding these two men together are intensely felt. Each defines himself through his opposite, and finds himself wanting. That is also why Rogozhin's feelings toward Myshkin shift so readily from love to hatred.

Immediately after this series of thoughts, Rogozhin makes an attempt on Myshkin's life. The sexual aspects of the attempted murder reinforce the basic elements of the relationship between the two men. Rogozhin attacks with a knife (we are not told whether or not it is *the* knife, but it is not crucial), an object which has been associated with his aggressive masculine sexuality. Myshkin's reaction to the attack is also sexual in a way; his epileptic seizure resembles a sexual climax, involving rhythmic physical convulsions, facial distortion, and a moment of pleasure so intense that it borders on pain.[9] Yet elsewhere in the novel this epilepsy has been a sign of the absence of sexuality in his personality, at least the absence of masculine sexuality. So the sexual imagery of this scene links the two men with masculine and feminine sex roles. As in *Notes from Underground*, sexual stereotypes come to stand for the aggressive-passive distinction so important throughout Dostoevsky's works. Sexual experience becomes a metaphor for a wide variety of human relationships.

In terms of plot, jealousy over Nastasya Filippovna motivates the murder attempt, but this jealousy only partially explains the attack. She is only a pretext; she represents one of the issues between them. Both want her, to be sure, but Rogozhin wants her body, while Myshkin wants her soul. This is the real issue: which is stronger—Rogozhin's physicality or Myshkin's spirituality? The struggle to influence and possess Nastasya Filippovna becomes a power struggle between the two men, and moreover, it is a contest between two sorts of power, the aggressive and the meek. Each is trying, through Nastasya Filippovna, to vindicate his own mode of relating to others; she becomes a means of resolving certain issues in their relationship with each other.[10]

Indeed, their identification with each other is so intense that they seem at times to be two halves of the same character. This is reinforced by the fact that each lacks the qualities possessed to excess by the other. In a sense, each is only half a person; each needs the other to become a complete human being. This possibility finds extraordinary confirmation in the rough drafts, where we find a character called "the idiot" who is remarkable for the extreme opposites present in his character. He vacillates between good and evil, between weakness and aggression. He is epileptic, like Myshkin, yet he commits rape and murder, crimes that only Rogozhin would be likely to commit in the final version.[11] It seems quite likely that the contradictions in the proposed character became too unwieldly and he was finally divided into two characters, Myshkin and Rogozhin. So the two men really are born of one person; they are two halves of the same personality.

Indeed, each of them does flirt with the possibilities represented by his alter ego. Myshkin is very interested in aggression as a phenomenon, specifically he is fascinated by murderers facing execution, that is, with aggressive men taking on the role of victim (see Chapter 8 for further discussion of this image). Further, his moody confusions, his inexplicable excitements and his self-deprecatory outburst before Rogozhin's murder attempt may be viewed as examples of aggression directed inward, something we have already seen in a different form in the underground man and others. Likewise, Rogozhin's vague connection with the Skoptsy, his servant-like role with Nastasya Filippovna in Part II, and the ultimately self-destructive direction of his passion, all suggest movement toward submissive traits. But all of these unrealized or partially realized traits serve only to underline their overall difference from each other.

Elizabeth Dalton interprets the novel in classic Freudian terms as an Oedipal triangle. Myshkin's attempt to take Nastasya Filippovna away from Rogozhin becomes the child's attempt to deny his parents' sexuality, and the murder attempt in II 5 becomes a reenactment of the 'primal scene' (child viewing parents' coitus) with Myshkin protectively taking the place of his father's love object.[12] This is a possible, even an ingenious, but not a necessary interpretation of the work. There is insufficient textual basis for seeing Rogozhin and Nastasya Filippovna as parent figures for Myshkin. In fact we can arrive at a much more universal interpretation of the novel, and still preserve many details of Dalton's Freudian interpretation, by adopting René Girard's concept of mimetic desire. In fact, the Oedipal triangle may be seen as the first instance of the mimetic triangle, in which the father is the admired and hated role model/competitor.[13] This provides us with a broader and more flexible interpretive framework, into which the Myshkin/Rogozhin/Nastasya Filippovna triangle readily fits. The rough drafts for *A Raw Youth* confirm the interchangeability of mimetic and Oedipal triangles. In the earliest drafts, Dostoevsky places his adolescent hero into a mimetic triangle with an older brother. Finally, it occurs to him "It will be better if it is his own FATHER!"[14]

The next time we see Rogozhin is when the two friends meet in the park on the eve of Myshkin's birthday party. Here their identity is stressed even further, and it is specifically connected with the attempted murder in Part 2. Myshkin says:

> "Now I know by heart what your state of mind was on that day [of the murder attempt], as though it were myself. . . . I had a premonition from the morning of that day, looking at you. . . . When we exchanged crosses, then perhaps, the thought began to stir in me. . . . We had exactly the same impulse at that time. If you had not raised your hand against me then, . . . what would I have been before you. Indeed, I suspected you anyway, our sin was the same, the very same." (III 3)

Thus their identity is stressed at the very moment the crime was conceived. The murderer and his victim both participate in the act of murder as two halves of a single whole.

This is further suggested by the following sentence describing the epileptic seizure: "[In epilepsy] it seems even that someone else within [the epileptic] is crying out." (II 5) And indeed a change does seem to be taking place in Myshkin. Immediately after their conversation in the park in Part 3, Myshkin invites Rogozhin to his birthday party: "I don't want to meet my new life without you. . . . Don't you know, Rogozhin, that my new life is beginning." Rogozhin agrees, and adds, "You're not yourself at all, Lyov Nikolaevich!" (III 3) During Part 3 Myshkin initiates several actions associated with a traditional masculine role: he prepares to fight a duel, takes up a fatherly attitude toward Ippolit,[15] and begins a romantic involvement with Aglaya Epanchina, although he has as low an opinion of his own sexual identity as ever. His close friendship with an opposite personality type (Rogozhin) coincides with his movement away from the extreme personality type he himself had represented at the opening of the novel.

But all of his manly projects end in disaster: Ippolit dies, the duel never comes off, and he makes an absolute mess of his "courtship" of Aglaya. Rogozhin likewise fails in his attempt to build a workable marriage relationship with Nastasya Filippovna. Both of these failures revert to the behavioral extremes they had represented at the outset.

In the grisly and beautiful final scene of the novel, Rogozhin insists that they make up a bed and sleep together in the presence of Nastasya Filippovna's corpse, even though this involves considerable difficulty. (IV 11) Thus their identity in the presence of Nastasya Filippovna's corpse becomes an almost physical identity, and this is given inordinate stress in the text, just as is the theme of the knife earlier. Once again, this highlights the issues of sexual identity involved in their friendship. In fact, these two characters, opposite yet complementary, seem to merge in this final scene, just as they may have emerged out of a single character in the creation of the novel. At last, Myshkin finds it difficult to distinguish his own personal identity:

> Finally [Myshkin] lay down on the pillow, as though completely helpless and despairing, and pressed his face against the pale and motionless face of Rogozhin. Tears flowed from his eyes onto Rogozhin's cheeks, but perhaps he could no longer even distinguish his own tears, and knew nothing about them. (IV 11)

One pictures a cubist face capturing profile and front view in a single circle. The two opposites, both having failed in their attempts to complete themselves and deal with the world beyond the self, have finally altogether lost the ability to distinguish between self and other.

The Eternal Husband was written immediately after *The Idiot,* and the romantic triangle in that novel is again an excellent illustration of the mimetic triangle. The two male characters, Trusotsky and Velchaninov, have shared the same woman, Trusotsky's late wife. Now that she is dead the cuckold and the paramour gravitate toward each other, a good example of the way in which, as Girard observes, the rival becomes more important psychologically than the love object itself.[16] Trusotsky introduces Velchaninov to his new prospective bride, and the latter alienates her affections. (XII) Later that night the wronged bridegroom attempts to murder his rival. (XV) The characters' actions seem unconsciously designed to perpetuate the triangular rivalry. Similar triangular relationships are important in the early works *The Landlady, White Nights,* "A Weak Heart" and "Another Man's Wife and a Husband under the Bed."

This sort of identification with opposites in Dostoevsky is not confined to masculine friendships, however. In the unfinished novel *Netochka Nezvanova* (1849) we find an early depiction of friendship between a proud girl and her quite companion. They identify intensely with each other and exchange days of personal mastery, exerting control sometimes through straightforward dominance and sometimes through submission. (V)[17]

A similar identification of opposites is apparent in the relationship between Nastasya Filippovna, the fallen woman, and Aglaya Epanchina, the young debutante. Nastasya writes a letter to her rival:

> "If I were even the slightest bit your equal, you might be offended by such impudence. But who am I, and who are you? We two are such opposites, and I am so completely beneath you, that I couldn't possibly offend you, even if I wanted to. . . . But nevertheless I am in love with you. Although love equalizes people, don't worry, I haven't put myself on a level with you, not even in my most private thoughts." (III 10)[18]

Aglaya correctly observes what seems at first glance to be contradictory: that this slavish adoration of her opposite demonstrates Nastasya's self-love. In fact the submissive posture taken in the letter is intended sarcastically and actually reveals Nastasya's rage and hatred toward Aglaya and a sense of offended self-esteem. What is interesting here is the fact that these emotions are encoded in the form of dominant-submissive relationships and adoration of opposites. The hostility soon becomes explicit, however, using the competition for Myshkin's love as a pretext.

> At last [Aglaya] looked directly and fixedly into Nastasya Filippovna's eyes and read clearly at that moment all that flashed in the malicious gaze of her rival. Each woman understood the other. . . . Both looked at each other, no longer concealing their malice. (IV 8)

(The whole scene reminds one of the meeting between Grushenka and Katerina in *The Brothers Karamazov,* in which open hostility is thinly masked by sugary sweet talk.) This particular set of relationships in *The Idiot* is symmetrical. There are two parallel love triangles here, centered around Nastasya Filippovna and Myshkin, and in each triangle the rivals are opposites whose close friendship borders on hostility.

The doubling in *Crime and Punishment, The Brothers Karamazov* and *The Devils* is parallel rather than contrastive. In the first, as critics have noted, Raskolnikov is doubled by both Sonya and Svidrigailov.[19] As his name suggests, Raskolnikov is an inwardly divided character; he has both an aggressive and a compassionate nature. These two external characters represent the opposing sides of his character. Svidrigailov is a predatory type and he stands for all that is aggressive in Raskolnikov. The meek Sonya represents Raskolnikov's urge to self-sacrifice.

In *The Brothers Karamazov,* Ivan's devil is a parallel double, echoing certain aspects of Ivan's personality and ideology, and visiting him only at night, since these are private sides of Ivan's character. (XI 9) Like the second Mr. Golyadkin in *The Double,* this devil is probably a figment of Ivan's imagination, hence an internal double. But Ivan's devil may also be likened to an external double, Zosima's mysterious nighttime visitor. The structure of their nocturnal visits is quite similar. Zosima's visitor echoes the pattern of repentance and salvation which is going on within the future monk, but represents the secret criminal which remains within his soul. (VI 2 d)

The relationships between Stavrogin and his friends Shatov, Kirillov and Pyotr Verkhovensky in *The Devils* are further instances of parallel doubling. Stavrogin is surrounded by characters each of whom echoes one of his traits and seems bound to him by this link. Each looks to Stavrogin for a definition of his own identity, and Stavrogin has enough contradictory elements in his own character to provide ample material for each of them in turn. But the contradictory elements in Stavrogin's personality balance each other to such a degree that he cannot propel himself emotionally in any one direction. Stavrogin's role in the novel is to produce ideas which arouse others to action and pursue them to destruction, but about which he himself is indifferent. The novel's epigraph and title refer to the New Testament parable of the man possessed by many demons whose exorcism causes a stampede of swine infected by his demons. Stavrogin is this demoniac, producing ideas which destroy others, but which leave him unmoved.[20]

It is this very coldness which attracts Kirillov to Stavrogin, for Kirillov believes that widespread indifference to life and death will bring an end to pain and usher in the age of the man-god. Of course, Kirillov misunderstands Stavrogin in a crucial way, for Stavrogin's indifference is a personal trait, while Kirillov's is a metaphysical concept. Kirillov is talking about the impassibility of man, his godlikeness, at the moment of death, when time ceases. (This reminds one of Myshkin's ecstatic vision preceding a seizure, and thus it is not surprising that Shatov asks if Kirillov is epileptic.) Stavrogin agrees with Kirillov's idea when it is explained to him, but he is unable to get as excited about the idea as Kirillov does. It is even hinted that Stavrogin is the author of this idea, or of some idea very important to

Kirillov. "Remember what you've meant in my life, Stavrogin," says Kirillov at the end of their first meeting recorded in the novel. (I 1 V) Shatov confirms this hint saying: "You fixed [Kirillov's] mind in falsehood and slander and brought him to the edge of insanity. Go, look at him now—he's your creation." (II 1 VII) This suggests that Kirillov's ideas may have originated with Stavrogin, and indeed Stavrogin seems to exemplify Kirillov's ideal of indifference. Kirillov's own suicide is intended to illustrate his principles, but Stavrogin's suicide seems to be a more perfect example of utter indifference to life or death, marred only by the greased rope, a calculated step to check any reflexive love of life at the last moment.

Stavrogin is also the author of Shatov's idée fixe, but it seems that Stavrogin had only been toying with Slavophile ideas when he inflamed Shatov with them.[21] (Shatov tries to remind him of these views:

> "If you have gone back on those words of yours about the people, how could you have brought yourself to utter them at that time? . . . Do you remember your expression, that . . . 'An atheist at once ceases to be a Russian? . . .' Didn't you tell me that if it were mathematically proved to you that truth was outside Christ, you would rather remain with Christ than with truth."

Stavrogin admits that in those words he recognizes his own mood two years ago, but he insists that his belief was not complete, even at the time: ". . . trying to convince you, I was perhaps even more concerned with myself than with you." (II 1 VII) Shatov could have picked up these Slavophile ideas anywhere; they were widely current at the time. The fact that he received them from Stavrogin produces an inordinate dedication to Slavophilism, because of his inordinate devotion to Stavrogin:

> "Stavrogin," he complains, "why am I condemned to believe in you forever and ever? Could I have spoken like this to anyone else? I am modest, but I was not afraid of my nakedness because I was speaking to Stavrogin. I was not afraid of caricaturing a great idea by my touch because Stavrogin was listening to me. . . . Don't you know that I shall kiss your footprints after you have gone? I can't tear you out of my heart, Nikolai Stavrogin." (II 1 VII)

But the tie between Shatov and Stavrogin is much more than an ideological one. In terms of ideology the doubling here is parallel, but in personal terms, it is contrastive, involving sexual jealousy and aggressive hostility, like the friendships between Myshkin and Rogozhin or Trusotsky and Velchaninov. Stavrogin has had an affair with Shatov's wife and very probably fathered the child she bears in the course of the novel. A liaison between

Stavrogin and Shatov's sister is also suggested. Like Myshkin and Rogo-zhin, then, the two men share the same woman. Another similarity with the friendship in *The Idiot* is the possibility of physical violence between the two friends. Shatov becomes convinced that Stavrogin is going to kill him and he buys a gun to protect himself. The assault expected here is by the dominant member of the relationship against his weaker friend, as in *The Idiot*. In fact, in the rough drafts it was the Stavrogin character who slapped the Shatov character.[22] But when a personal assault actually takes place, it is Shatov who strikes Stavrogin, in the last chapter of Part 1.

Stavrogin is remarkably powerful, dominating practically everyone he comes in contact with, but in public behavior he exhibits a desire to humiliate himself dramatically, to undercut his own powerful position by placing himself in a position of weakness. He tells Kirillov as they discuss suicide:

> "I can understand wanting to shoot oneself, of course. . . . I've imagined it myself sometimes, and then always a new idea occurred to me; if one were to commit a crime, or something shameful, that is, something really disgraceful, that's the main thing—it should be something very mean and—ridiculous, so that people would remember it for a thousand years and remember it with disgust for a thousand years. . ." (II 1 V)

This type of inversion in the dominance hierarchy is typical of the strong central figures of the late novels, particularly Stavrogin and Versilov (see Chapter 8).

The most complicated of all these friendships is the relationship between Stavrogin and Pyotr Verkhovensky. The latter wants to capitalize on Stavrogin's awe-inspiring personality, mkaing him the figurehead leader of his international political conspiracy.

> ". . . I love an idol. You are my idol! . . . You are just the type that is needed! I, yes I need just such a one as you. I know no one but you. You are the leader; you are the sun, and I am a worm before you. . . ." He suddenly kissed [Stavrogin's] hand. . . . "Why are you looking at me that way? I need you, yes you. Without you I am nothing, an idea in a bottle, Columbus without America." (II 8)

Of course Verkhovensky's devotion is not so disinterested as is Shatov's. Verkhovensky worships Stavrogin, but his apparently self-abnegating obeisance is actually an attempt to manipulate this idol, to become the power behind the power:

> "Listen, I won't show you to anyone, not to anyone. It must be so. 'He exists, but no one has seen him. He is in hiding.' Perhaps I can show you to one out of a hundred thousand, you know. And he will travel all over the world, announcing, 'We have seen him, we have seen him.'" (II 8)

we have only his word for all of this. As it becomes patently obvious that his attempts to dominate her spring from his own insecurities, we begin to wonder if perhaps she is not so meek a creature as he imagines. In any case the situation unquestionably chganges from one in which he dominates, if only by virtue of age and financial superiority, to one in which she has the upper hand.

Finally, in the chapter entitled "The Gentle Girl Revolts," he tells us that she is behaving "completely out of character, one might even say she had reversed her character. She was a wild creature, aggressive and, I cannot say shameless, but improper, and seeking occasions to rebel." (I 5) She has an affair with an old army pal of his, who reveals to her all of the humiliating circumstances surrounding her husband's expulsion from the regiment. The narrator observes their meeting through a keyhole and sees a very different woman than the one he has imagined her to be. He still interprets her actions as springing from meek and girlish naïveté, morally superior to the aggresive male who is assailing her, but he finds that she is quite able to take care of herself.

> "I was present for a whole hour at this duel between a noble and elevated woman with a perverted, wordly and dull-witted creature, an utterly cringing soul. And where, I wondered, hurt, had this naive, this gentle, this quiet girl learned all of this." (I 5)

He bursts in on them and takes her home, but he does not accept her would-be lover's flippant and insulting challenge to a duel, nor does he punish or even scold her, as she seems to expect:

> ". . . she fixed me with a penetrating gaze. She was extremely pale, her lips formed a mocking smile, but she looked at me then with a triumphant and stern challenge, and it seemed that she was seriously convinced that I would kill her with a revolver . . ." (I 5)

The phrase "stern challenge" is especially significant here: "stern" is the word which was used to describe the husband's attitude immediately after the marriage, while "challenge" describes the action of the disappointed lover at the interrupted rendezvous. The meek creature has "rebelled" and taken on the aggressive attitude appropriate, in the narrator's opinion, to the male. Neither speaks; he retires on their bed while she goes to sleep on the couch.

He awakens to find her standing over him with revolver at his temple. ". . . there was a battle going on between us at that very moment, a frightful, life-and-death duel. . . ." (I 6) She has replaced her paramour as her husband's opponent in a duel. He hopes to overcome her by passive resistance: ". . . if she had guessed the truth and knew that I was not asleep, then I had already crushed her with my readiness to accept death, and her hand might then falter." (I 6) Having no chance to hear her side of the story, we cannot verify his impression, but this is his attitude when she does not pull the trigger: "I was victorious, and she was forever conquered." He feels that he has triumphed, but he has done so by taking a passive role, meekly accepting the possibility of death at her hands. He buys her a separate bed, signifying that he decrees the end of their physical union, and apparently forgetting that she had initiated this by sleeping on the couch the previous night. "There was no longer any doubt," he says, using a phrase similar to the one used earlier to describe his power over her when his sexual interest in her was first aroused. Now the phrase is used to describe the end of their sexual union, and to describe what he sees as his attainment of full power over her, but what to the reader certainly looks like the opposite.

In the second part of the story, after a long illness, she takes up an attitude of complete indifference, ignoring him completely. When he realizes this he is filled, strangely, with ecstasy rather than disappointment. He makes a sexual advance which she meets with "stern surprise," and the word "stern," used earlier to describe the husband's attitude, is even italicized. (II 2) Her "sternness" seems to redouble his ecstasy.

> ". . . more and more unrestrained became my desires to lie again at her feet and again to kiss, to kiss the earth on which her feet stood, and to beg of her and—'I ask nothing, nothing from you any longer . . . do not answer my questions, take no notice of me at all, but only let me look at you from my corner, turn me into your object, your lap dog . . .'" (II 2)

She is unwilling to accept the life together that he proposes, it is not altogether clear whether because of disgust for his enjoyment of humiliation, shame over her own unfaithfulness, or distaste for a physical relationship with a man she does not respect. In any case, she kills herself and the whole story is her husband's monologue immediately after her death.[4]

The narrator of this work provides an extreme example of the pathological sexual atittudes which are so fundamental to Dostoevsky's view of the human condition. It is interesting to compare him with the underground man in this regard, since he exhibits many of the same problems, but presents a later stage in Dostoevsky's thinking. Like the underground man, he has been emphatically rejected by his male peers, and like the underground man he feels a strong physical attraction toward downtrodden and victimized women. Relationships with such women offer these men a chance to feel superior, to dominate, to direct elsewhere the humiliation they have received from their male superiors. Both men experience a tendency to see these sexual relationships inverted, with the wronged woman achieving a degree of mastery. But while the underground man saw this inversion as an occasion for a new sadistic reversal, the hero of "A Gentle Girl" carries to new heights the voluptuous delight in his humiliation at the hands of the offended woman. This complex of relationships and emotions encapsulates Dostoevsky's view of sexual relationships, or at least the extreme negative pole of that view. This situation is echoed in various ways throughout his works. One recalls, for instance, the almost comic scene in *Crime and Punishment* in which the drunken Marmeladov shouts as his wife drags him around the room by the hair in the presence of visitors, "This is pleasure for me! This is not painful, but ple-e-e-asure!" (I 2)

The same issues appear in *The Idiot* in the lovers' quadrangle, Rogozhin, Nastasya Filippovna, Myshkin and Aglaya. Nastasya Filippovna's background certainly puts her in the class of victimized women. After the death of her parents she was brought up by a guardian, old enough to be her father, who made her his mistress. This pattern of sexual oppression is well established, but one would hardly call Nastasya Filippova a meek or gentle creature. Here the inversion in which the downtrodden woman takes control takes place early. Nastasya Filippovna sets out to avenge the wrongs which have been done her, and in the early chapters of the novel she puts Totsky, her former guardian and lover, in a very tight spot. She also seems to revel in her power over her suitor Ganya Ivolgin, toying with him like a predatory animal as she first agrees to marry him and then thinks better of it. Finally she humiliates him decisively by throwing the money she has recieved from Rogozhin into the fire and goading Ganya into dragging it out.

Later in the novel she treats Rogozhin like a footman, despite all of his aggressive bluster. He complains to Myshkin:

> "She's on her way to the altar with me, but she's put me completely out of her thoughts, as though she were changing a shoe. Do you believe it, I haven't seen her for five days, because I don't dare go to her. She'll ask, 'Why have you come? . . .' She looks upon me as the most absolute rubbish." (II 3)

Nastasya Filippova herself makes this telling analogy concerning their relationship:

> ". . . there was once a certain pope, and he got angry with a certain emperor, who knelt barefoot for three days in front of the pope's palace, not eating or drinking, until the pope granted his absolution. What do

you think did that emperor, kneeling there for three days, think the whole thing over and make any vows to himself . . . to get revenge on the pope? . . . And you, perhaps you're making vows that: 'If she marries me, then I'll get back at her, then I'll enjoy myself at her expense.'" (II 3)

Here Rogozhin's physical dominance is likened to that of an emperor while Nastasya Filippovna's power is compared with that of a church leader. Her power, containing passive and spiritual elements, is stronger, in a sense, than the physical revenge that may be within Rogozhin's grasp.

Myshkin is as much attracted to victimized women as are other Dostoevskian men, but his sexuality is so completely repressed that this attraction does not have the prurient element here that it has with the others. Yet the structure of the bond between Myshkin and Nastasya Filippova is the same as in these other relationships: the vicimized woman comes to dominate the man who loves and feels compassion for her. Myshkin, in fact, is controlled by whomever he pities, and the most agonizing moment of decision comes for him when he is faced by two such women:

> Both [Nastasya Filippova] and Aglaya looked at the prince as though crazed. But he . . . only saw before him the despairing, insane face [of Nastasya], by which "his heart had been pierced forever," as he had once told Aglaya. He could bear it no longer and, with a plea and a reproach, turned to Aglaya, pointing at Nastasya Filippovna: "How can you! She is . . . so wretched!" But he had barely managed to utter these words when he fell silent under Aglaya's terrible gaze. In this gaze was expressed so much suffering, and at the same time such infinite hatred, that he wrung his hands, cried out and rushed to her, but it was already too late. (IV 8)

The victimized woman who controls by arousing pity has a field day with Myshkin, since compassion is an emotion which consumes him entirely. His relationship with Nastasya does not work since each pities the other too much, for Myshkin is also a somewhat pathetic figure. The Dostoevskian power balance is based on an inequality of power or at least a differentiation into spiritual and physical modes of power. Both Myshkin and Nastasya Filippovna exercise their control over each other in fundamentally the same way, by arousing compassion, and as a result, their relationship suffers from a power vacuum.

A comparable power vacuum exists in *The Insulted and the Injured.* The weakwilled young Alyosha Valkovsky reminds us slightly of Myshkin, with his fair hair and dreamy blue eyes, and his wife Natasha exercises dominion over him by sacrificing herself to him. (Chapter 9)

Crime and Punishment is filled with sexual oppression. Raskolnikov's sister Dunya is vicimtized by Svidrigailov and Luzhin, and, like Nastasya

Filippovna, she is able to turn the tables and gain the upper hand over both of them. Both men are prototypical Dostoevskian sexual villains. Svidrigailov's voluptuous dreams in the last few hours of his life make his predilection for sexual advances toward young girls unmistakably clear and even suggest that he once raped an adolescent girl, causing her suicide. (VI 6) This exactly parallels the excised chapter of *the Devils* where Stavrogin reveals that he has a similar crime on his conscience. Luzhin is equally predatory. His unsuccessful attempt to calumniate Sonya is an attempt to soothe his frustration after his designs on Dunya have been foiled. (V 3)

These subplots echo the theme of sexual power imbalance, but that theme is present in the primary plot as well, in Raskolnikov's murder of Lizaveta and the relationship with Sonya which leads him to repentance. Raskolnikov cannot come under the domination of the woman he has victimized, Lizaveta, since she is dead, but the close identification between Lizaveta and Sonya accomplishes the equivalent when he comes under Sonya's influence.

Sonya Marmeladova is the prototypical victimized young woman in the novel,[5] perhaps in Dostoevsky's work generally. She is forced by circumstances to become a professional prostitute, to make a living by submitting to the sexual domination of men. But Lizaveta, Sonya' equally meek and downtrodden friend, is also a submissive victim of sexual advances. Here is the opinion of an unnamed student: "She has such a kind face and eyes. Really quite kind. That's why many find her appealing. She's such a quiet girl, gentle, meek, agreeable, she'll agree to anything. And her smile is really quite pretty." (I 6) What particularly amuses the student is that Lizaveta is always pregnant, a dramatic symbol of her meek acceptance of sexual oppression. In the rough drafts, Lizaveta actually bears a child.[6]

Sonya and Lizaveta are linked in other ways as well. After the murder, Raskolnikov discovers that the two women used to meet to read and discuss the *New Testament,* and he uses the term "holy fool" (*yurodivy*) to describe both of them. Both are particularly noted for their childlike responses. For Sonya this childlike quality is particularly evident in the first meeting with Raskolinikov's mother and sister.

> "Seeing the room unexpectedly full of people she was not just embarrassed, but lost her nerve completely and became timid as a little child, and even began to go back out again . . . In spite of her 18 years she almost seemed a littlie girl yet, much younger than her years, almost a complete child . . ." (III 4)

Lizaveta's childlike reactions are especially vivid in the murder scene:

> . . . Her lips were twisted so piteously, as with very small children when they begin to be frightened, look intently at the object which frightens them and prepare to cry out, . . . [Lizaveta] only very slightly raised her unoccupied left hand, not up to her face at all, but slowly stretched it forward toward [Raskolnikov] as though pushing him away." (I 1)

Lizaveta is the link between Sonya and the murder. The two women are so closely linked that it seems as though Raskolnikov has murdered Sonya herself. In fact Sonya's reactions, and his own feelings, during the confession to Sonya, remind Raskolnikov and the reader of the murder scene.

> This minute was horribly similar in [Raskolnikov's] sensations, to the moment when he stood over the old woman . . . He looked at [Sonya] and suddenly it was as though he saw in her face the face of Lizaveta. [Here the narrator reminds the reader of Lizaveta's response to the attack.] Almost exactly the same thing happened now with Sonya. For a brief moment she looked at him just as helplessly, with her left hand forward and very lightly touched his chest with her fingers and slowly began to rise from the bed, steadily moving away from him as her eyes became steadily more fixed upon him." (IV 4)

Sonya's identification with Lizaveta enables us to see in *Crime and Punishment* the same pattern noted above in other works: a man commits an act of aggression against a victimized woman, and later comes under the moral influence of that woman, or as in this case, of her double. Throughout the novel Raskolnikov alternates between aggressive impulses and desires to protect wronged women. In I 4, he tries to protect a tipsy woman who is being pursued by a lecherous gentleman, then suddenly gives up in disgust.

Peace has noted that the division between passive and aggressive types in the novel underscores the division in Raskolnikov's own character.[7] His crime is a complicated one. It is an aggressive attack on a victimized individual, but it sets out to be a defense of such individuals from their oppressors. Raskonikov is at once on both sides of this dichotomy. Setting out to champion the downtrodden, he himself becomes their oppressor. Setting out to free himself from the bonds of law, he finds himself more in bondage than ever. This is illustrated by his emotional reaction when he learned of the coincidence, which will enable him to commit the murder: "He entered his room like one condemned to death . . . With his whole being he felt that his mind and will were no longer free and that everything was conclusively decided." (I 5) Raskolnikov renders himself powerless through his act of murderous aggression, and is only able to redeem himself through submission to the victim of that act (or, more exactly, to a stand-in for her). In a power inversion quite typical of Dostoevsky's work, the aggressor submits to the power of his victim. This submission is symbolized first when he bows to Sonya and kisses her boot during their first private interview. The sexual aspects of this submission are not made as explicit here as in other works, but they are strongly implied. Raskolnikov is after all "courting" Sonya, and these interviews take place in the very room, and sometimes on the very bed, where she received her gentlemen callers.

Not only does Raskolnikov submit to the moral power of his victim, Sonya/Lizaveta; he also identifies himself with their role as passive sufferers by taking upon himself several religious objects associated with them. He suspects from the first interview that this may happen when he says: "I too shall become a holy fool (yurodivy). It's infectious." (III 4) Sonya reads him the story of Lazarus out of Lizaveta's New Testament, and when he finally confesses to Sonya, she gives him her own cross to wear, while she herself puts on one that had belonged to Lizaveta. Thus, by confessing his crime he identifies himself with his victim and takes on her role of passive sufferer.[8] Such is the spiritual power of the submissive victim in Dostoevsky's moral system that upon his confession Sonya bows to him just as he had to her earlier. By imitating Sonya's submissiveness, Raskolnikov gains the power paradoxically conferred by such submissiveness, as Blackmur has noted.[9]

The relations between men and women in Dostoevsky's world are closely connected with the drama of violent crime and repentance. The aggressive male typically victimizes a childlike woman but in the aftermath of his crime submits to her domination and even identifies with her in the role of passive victim.

CHAPTER 7

GUILT, COMPASSION, AND THE POWER OF WEAKNESS

As has already been suggested, the best capsule version of Dostoevsky's ontological and moral system is the short story "The Dream of a Ridiculous Man." Not only does the narrator of that story express feelings of alienation which are psychologically, even philosophically, solipsistic; he also resolves his ontological doubts through a progression which is paradigmatically Dostoevskian. The fact that the character finally establishes contact with the world outside is evidence of an optimism which is rare in Dostoevsky's earlier work, and makes the story a fitting prelude to the epiphanies of *The Brothers Karamazov*.

As noted earlier, the hero-narrator of the story is unable to come to terms with the world outside himself, and he expresses his alienation by making himself "ridiculous" in the eyes of others, and by his occasional doubts about the reality of other minds. His emotional isolation reaches a peak when he is unable to feel pity for a starving, freezing, orphan girl, the victim *qua* victim. That night he dreams that he commits suicide. Self-inflicted death is an escape for him from the responsibilities of being fully human. (His suicide calls to mind Kirillov's doctrine of cosmic indifference.) After extinguishing his own being, he encounters a being outside himself. He reacts just as with his fellow human beings in earthly life—he assumes that the other rejects him: "You know that I fear you, and therefore you despise me." he says, feeling his humiliation "like the stabbing of a pin" in his heart. (III) But at last he perceives that the silent being does not despise him. As the being deposits him on a planet exactly like ours, its double (*dvoinik*) in fact, he feels the first stirrings of emotion and even remembers the hungry little girl. At first he is unwilling to accept his world because of its lack of the pain which binds him nostalgically to the one he has just left: "Is there torment in this new world? In our world we can only love with torment and through torment. . . . I want torment in order to love." (III) He soon discovers that this is the one difference between their world and ours—they have no knowledge of evil, no sin, no pain. Their planet is a genuine garden of Eden.

> "Although they knew a great deal, they did not have our science. But I soon understood that their knowledge was supplied and nourished by different impulses than ours on earth and that their desires were also completely different. . . . They did not desire to comprehend life, for their lives were full. . . . Our science seeks to explain the nature of life

. . . in order to teach others how to live. They know without science how they ought to live." (III)

The parallels with *Genesis* and *Notes from Underground* are clear. It is the knowledge of good and evil, the disease of self-consciousness, that brings about evil. Like the rest of their lives, their sexuality is without cruelty. He goes on: "They had love and they gave birth to children, but I never noticed outbursts in them of that *cruel*[1] voluptuousness which is the sole source of almost all of the sins of our humanity." (IV)

But this state of innocence does not last long once the narrator of the story arrives. He corrupts them and the result is that they become alienated from one another. They develop science and the full panoply of human vices as a result of their acquaintance with their earthly visitor. And their corrupter, through a sense of his own guilt, pities and loves them even more, and seeks to expiate his guilt through punishment at their hands.

The hero awakens to find himself once again in our world (although the two worlds should be now fully identical since he has introduced evil into the other one). The result is that he now lives in a world full of sin and pain with the consciousness of having caused that sin and that pain. This guilt provides a point of contact with the world outside himself; through guilt and the pity it arouses, he establishes a connection with the nonself. He finds the little girl again. When he first encountered her he could feel no compassion since there was no link between himself and her pain. Now such a link exists; he can feel pity for a victimized creature in pain only if he can see that he himself is the cause of that pain. And through this guilt-induced pity he is finally able to built a relationship with the world around him. Acceptance of personal guilt is the way out of psychological solipsism for Dostoevsky's psychopathic characters.[2]

Ivan Karamazov's behavior with the drunken and freezing peasant is paradigmatically similar to the basic structure of "The Dream of a Ridiculous Man." Before Smerdyakov's confession, which implicates Ivan and gives rise to a sense of guilt, Ivan is willing to let the man freeze. After he accepts his own guilt, Ivan expends considerable effort to see that the man gets medical attention. In both cases, the acceptance of personal guilt is the bridge between the solipsistic character and the world beyond himself.

This connection between pity and guilt also provides the key to the extraordinary power wielded in Dostoevsky's works by characters who are weak, victimized, or vulnerable in a variety of ways. Vulnerability produces pity, pity in turn arouses feelings of guilt, and once that has taken place the victimized character has one of the most powerful of human emotions as a means of maintaining control. Usually this takes place unconsciously, but a few characters, like Nastasya Filippovna wield it openly with full awareness of its power. Vulnerability may be produced in a variety of ways in Dostoevsky's works, but it always gives a peculiar sort of moral or spiritual power to the vulnerable character, achieved through the arousal of guilt in his or her interlocutor. Young women are always vulnerable in Dostoevsky's works (Varvara in *Poor Folk*), especially if they are sexually oppressed (Sonya Marmedladova). Children have this quality (Ilyusha Snegirev in *The Brothers Karamazov*) as does anyone childlike (Lizaveta).[3] Meek characters (the heroine of "A Gentle Girl") and religious people (the Bible saleswoman or Maria Lebyadkina in *the Devils*) have this feature. Womanish men assume this characteristic of vulnerability along with their femininity (Porfiry Petrovich in *Crime and Punishment*), as does any man lacking in sexual vigor (Myshkin). Characters facing imminent death (Ippolit in *The Idiot*), feeble-minded characters (the Swiss girl Marie in *The Idiot*), poor people (Pokrovsky in *Poor Folk*) and drunkards (Marmeladov in *Crime and Punishment*) should be included. Sometimes this vulnerability is overdetermined, as in the case of the Swiss girl Marie (*The Idiot*) who possesses practically all of the determinants of vulnerability. Characters who possess it form a special class and wield a special power.

Using anthropological terminology, one might say that vulnerability is totemic in Dostoevsky's world. Freud describes the totem animal in primitive societies as an animal to which special magical power (*mana*) is attributed. The veneration of this animal is basic to the tribe's sense of identity, both as a group and as individuals. The strongest taboo is placed on the killing of the totem animal, and this taboo arises out of a feeling of guilt which is basic to the development of the tribe's collective superego, its sense of social right and wrong. In fact, this sense of guilt, and the totemistic system which arises out of it, is the basis of social organization in the tribe.[4]

If we look at the characters who people Dostoevsky's novels as a special population, as a tribe, we find that all of these statements apply to the victimized or vulnerable character. We find that the worst kind of villainy imaginable in this little society is an offense practiced against such an innocent victim. This strong proscription results from guilt associated with the domination of the weak by the strong. And yet such hierarchical differentiation of power roles seems to be basic to concepts of personal and collective identity, fundamental to social organization as well. The vulnerable victim, the totem of this Dostoevskian tribe, attains through all of this an extraordinary sort of spiritual power, since the guilt he or she produces is the foundation of personal identity and social conscience.

For Freud, of course, the totemic victim is the tyrannical father of the patriarchal horde, the highest ranking figure in the dominance hierarchy rather than the lowest ranking. But Freud notes the interchangeability of these opposites in the hierarchy by suggesting that the primal father was probably replaced as leader by his *youngest* son.[5] René Girard also notes that the sacrifical victim must be low-ranking and innocent and, similarly, Mikhail Bakhtin points out that these two roles are reversed in the selection of a low-ranking figure as carnival king.[6]

This is nowhere better illustrated than in *The Brothers Karamazov* where the concept of violence to children is central to the dynamics of the novel. This concept provides the basis for Ivan's rejection of Christianity, functioning as the most heinous sin which stands for all sin. (II 5 IV) The centrality of this concept is the reason for Liza Khokhlakova's voluptuous delight in her fantasies about it. She imagines herself calmly eating fruit compote while watching the crucifixion of a child. Shortly after this, though, she punishes herself for this fantasy, by deliberately slamming a door on her finger. (III 11 III) In doing this she is imitating Alyosha Karamazov, whose finger has previously been bitten by the chief offended child in the novel, Ilyusha Snegiryov. Symbolically, then, she is receiving her punishment from the offended child himself. It is the totemic status of the victim that produces the "powerful weaklings" of Dostoevsky's novels and the inversions of the power balance that abound there. A case in point is Marya Lebyadkina (actually Stavrogina) in *The Devils*. Lame, insane and downtrodden, she has virtually all of the determinants of "totemic vulnerability." And yet she exercises a certain degree of power. She treats her bullying brother Lebyadkin "like a footman," although he beats her for it. She initiates the action of the entire novel by her trip to the cathedral where she bows down before Mrs. Stavrogina (the other one) and begs to kiss her hand. (I 4 IVI) This is an act of formal submission which puts her briefly in control of the scene and gives her considerable power over Mrs. Stavrogina. Such bows form a recurring paradigm in Dostoevsky's late works, particularly in *The Brothers Karamazov*. (See Chapter 9)

The reader shares the bafflement of the other characters over Stavrogin's secret marriage to Marya. When Stavrogin reveals his yearning for self-degradation, this seems to partially explain the marriage, but a fuller explanation comes to light in Stavrogin's confession to Tikhon, a chapter which is often omitted since the censor cut it from the original version. Here we discover that Stavrogin is guilty of the seduction and, in effect, the murder of a little girl. Unquestionably, then, his feelings of pity for Marya Lebyadkina, a wronged and childlike woman, are related to his strong feelings of guilt. His marriage to Marya relates to the earlier crime in two opposing, yet oddly complementary ways. It is a reenactment of the crime, for the relationship with Marya, a wronged and childlike woman, has the same structure as the liaison with the little girl. The marriage is totemic in the manner described by Freud. By protecting Marya as a substitute for his earlier victim he also protects himself from his guilt. But he is at the same time punishing himself by this degrading marriage beneath his station.

During his one scene alone with Marya, she treats him as a servant and calls him a pretender, although she recognizes the possibility that he may murder her. (II 2 III) This is once again a confrontation between physical and spiritual power. When his actions do result in her being murdered, his guilt overwhelms him. As he is taking leave of Liza Drozdova, he says, "If you hear anything in the near future, Liza, you should know, I'm guilty." (III 3 I) His protection of Marya protected him from his guilt over the earlier crime. When Marya is murdered, indirectly by him, his guilt for both crimes merges and engulfs him.

In *The Idiot* there is particular fascination with characters who are vulnerable because they face imminent death. The possibility that Nastasya Filippovna will die under Rogozhin's knife is one of the reasons she so enthralls Myshkin. The four descriptions of convicts facing execution echo this concern. (see Chapter 8)

But the most important character in the novel who faces imminent death is Ippolit Terentev. The fact of his consumptive condition defines his position in the novel. He controls other characters by arousing their sympathy. In Part II, Chapter 9 he has just outraged everyone by his obnoxious defense of the nihilists' demands, but he suddenly converts them all into sympathetic friends by coughing up blood. The power balance is inverted and the pathetic character takes charge. "Excuse me for giving orders," he says, as he directs Myshkin to serve them all tea. The transformation is most vivid in Lizaveta Prokofevna Epanchina, who goes from a vociferous paroxysm of rage to taking Ippolit under her wing. (II 9) At Myshkin's birthday party Ippolit again takes center stage in similar fashion with his "explanation" and attempted suicide. (III 5-7) He controls these scenes by being pathetic, and although he does not do so consciously, the effect he produces is no less strong because of it. In the same novel, Myshkin repeatedly achieves control of a scene by allowing himself to be humiliated.[7]

Two Dostoevskian "weaklings" who quite consciously manipulate the "power of weakness" are Pyotr Verkhovensky in *The Devils* (*The Possessed*) and Porfiry Petrovich, the detective in *Crime and Punishment*. Verkhovensky's machinations have already been described in Chapter 5. In *Crime and*

Punishment, the hardly intimidating detective is described thus:

> Porfiry Petrovich was dressed for staying at home in, a dressing gown, spotless linen and well-worn slippers. He was a man of about 35, somewhat shorter than average, plump, even pot-bellied, clean-shaven, with neither mustache nor sideburns, with close-cropped hair on his large round head. . . . His chubby, round and somewhat snub-nosed face was a sickly yellowing color, but was fairly . . . kind, except for the expression of the eyes, with a sort of liquid, watery gleam, covered with almost white, twitching eyelids, as though he were winking at someone. The look of these eyes was in strange disharmony with his whole figure, which even had a certain womanish quality. . . . (III 5)

Porfiry Petrovich pursues Raskolnikov by befriending him and insisting always that he is not under suspicion. Yet at the crucial moment he always drops a hint that the exact opposite is the case. Giving an impression of mild-mannered and bumbling incompetence, he puts Raskolnikov off his guard. Appearing to be interested in trivial and peripheral details he will suddenly pounce upon the chief matter of suspicion. This cat-and-mouse game drives Raksolnikov to distraction and puts him utterly in the power of Porfiry Petrovich.[8]

Porfiry and Pyotr are able to control through apparent weakness because of the inversion of the straightforward power balance typical of Dostoevsky's works. This is possible because of the mysterious, totemic power of the vulnerable character in Dostoevsky's works. The wronged child, or a comparable victimized character, defines the Dostoevskian community as its totem. The crime against such a victim is the ultimate crime in this community, and just such a primal crime seems to be the basis of the guilt which underlies the Dostoevskian code of social behavior. Acceptance of this guilt provides escape from the solipsistic box in which the Dostoevskian psychopath (the underground man, the ridiculous man) finds himself trapped.

CHAPTER 8

THE CRIMINAL AS VICTIM

The victimized or vulnerable character, as we have seen, becomes a special repository of moral power in Dostoevsky's world. In anthropological terms, he or she is a bearer of strong "mana." Violence to this "totemized" victim becomes the fundamental taboo in Dostoevsky's system of social ethics, and as a result, scenes of such violence become pivotal in the action of the novels.

Over against the victimized character is his or her tormentor, the tyrannical character, who either achieves redemption by imitating his victim's submission (Raskolnikov), directs his violence against himself (Svidrigailov) or retires in defeat (Luzhin). The polarity between these two extreme types is the axis along which the drama of Dostoevsky's novels unfolds.

But in several of the major novels we encounter characters who combine characteristics from both ends of this polarity. The example which immediately springs to mind is Stavrogin, the central character in *The Devils*. His personal charisma is such that other characters defer to him immediately and almost reflexively. His dominance in the community is unquestioned and automatic. The characters who are in his thrall include Shatov, Kirillov, Pyotr Verkhovensky, Fedka, Lebyadkin, Marya Lebyadkina, Liza Drozdova, Dasha Shatova, and Marie Shatova. Testimonials of their devotion include the following:

> Shatov: "Stavrogin, why am I condemned to believe in you forever? . . . Isn't it true that I'll kiss your footprints when you've gone? I can't tear you out of my heart. . . ." (II 1 VII)
> Kirillov: "Remember what you have meant in my life, Stavrogin." (II 1 V)
> Pyotr Verkhovensky: "You are my idol. . . . You are the leader, you are the sun, and I am a worm before you. . . ." (II 8)
> Fedka: "I think I'd be better off bowing down to a boot [i.e., the nobleman Stavrogin] than to a [peasant's] bast shoe." (II 2 I)
> Lebyadkin: ". . . you are the master here, not I. I am, so to speak, only acting as your steward . . ." (II 2 II)
> Liza: "I will follow you to the ends of the earth . . . like a dog." (III 3 II)

But his dominance in his peer group is also unsolicited; he longs, in fact, for humiliation and a lower position in the hierarchy. His comment to Kirillov, already quoted in Chapter 5, bears repeating: "I can understand wanting to shoot oneself, of course . . . I've imagined it myself sometimes, and then always a new idea occurred to me; if one were to commit a crime, or something shameful, that is, something really disgraceful, that's the main thing; it should be something very mean and—ridiculous, so that people would remember it for a thousand years and remember it with disgust for a thousand years. . . ." (II 1 V)

A number of incidents in his past may be interpreted as attempts to humiliate himself in this fashion. But unlike Raskolnikov or the underground man, who alternate between aggressive and submissive behavior, Stavrogin's efforts at self-humiliation are inextricably bound up with his sadistic aggressiveness.[1] Biting the governor's ear and pulling Gaganov's nose are aggressive acts, but silly ones, designed to humiliate the aggressor more than the victim. In his duel with Gaganov the younger, actions which would be seen as cowardly and humiliating for any other character are viewed as the arrogant actions of a bully coming from Stavrogin. He allows himself to be repeatedly insulted by a man who wants a pretext for a duel, he tries to avoid the duel by apologizing profusely for every imagined insult, and he even tries to effect a reconciliation as the duel is beginning. So powerful is Stavrogin's public image that his "cowardly" behavior is interpreted by Gaganov as a fresh insult: ". . . such concessions only increase the insult! He doesn't think it is possible to be insulted by me! He doesn't find it disgraceful to run away from me at the barrier! Who does he take me for after that. . . ." (II 3 II) Even Stavrogin's attempts at public weakness increase his public strength. Furthermore, by facing Gaganov's bullet unprotected he engages in self-destructive behavior which is again interpreted as arrogant and insulting.

His marriage to Marya Lebyadkina may be viewed as the sexual tyranny of a bully over a defenseless girl, yet it is also a product of his will to self-abasement. By marrying a half-wit with no social position he places into his closet a humiliating skeleton which hounds him throughout the novel. But his greatest and most guilty secret is his rape (probably statutory) of a young girl and her consequent suicide. This has exactly the same structure as his relations with Marya Lebyadkina: his behavior is aggresive, even sadistic, but the impulse behind that behavior is partially masochistic; it derives from a desire to humiliate or even destroy himself.[2] In his "Confession" he states:

> "Every extremely disgraceful, boundlessly humiliating, base and, most important, ridiculous situation in which I have happened to be during my life has always aroused in me, along with boundless anger, incredible pleasure . . . I like the ecstasy of the agonizing consciousness of my baseness." ("At Tikhon's," II)

He notes the presence of this feeling at times of criminal behavior, danger, while waiting for his opponent to fire in a duel, when receiving a slap, and finally:

> ". . . If the French vicomte, who struck me on the cheek when I was abroad, and whose lower jaw I shot off for it, had grabbed me by the hair and forced me to kneel, perhaps I would have felt this rapture and maybe I wouldn't have felt any anger." ("At Tikhon's," II)

The genesis of the Stavrogin character lies in the continuing plans for "The Life of a Great Sinner," which was never actually written, but which lies behind all of the novels of the seventies. The concept of tremendous innate strength seeking suffering is present from the beginning of these drafts. The "great sinner" wants everyone to bow before him and he demands for himself either "boundless despotism or slavery." As these notebooks become *The Devils,* Stavrogin slaps the character who will become Shatov, but the act is seen as a "spiritual burden" (*podvig*). Thus the slap maintains a balance of aggressive and self-abnegating components. It is suggested that Stavrogin may join the Skoptsy, a flagellant sect, which maintained a rigid dominance hierarchy and practiced self-castration.[3] This sect is also mentioned prominently in connection with Rogozhin, suggesting that this sort of self-mutilation was an option even for him.

Thus it is the combination of sadistic and masochistic characteristics, not merely an alternation but a simultaneous admixture of aggression and vulnerability in each of his acts, which makes Stavrogin so puzzling and so charismatic. To some extent this is merely intentional mystification, a novelist's trick, and it has irritated a good many readers.[4] But even so it is a trick which unites qualities from both ends of Dostoevsky's most fundamental polarity and as such it is a significant link in his overall system.[5]

Versilov in *The Adolescent* (*A Raw Youth*) is a less successful attempt to bring together victim and tyrant. The humiliating elements are the same: an embarrassing marriage and an unavenged slap. Like Stavrogin, Versilov possesses a charismatic dominance which is immediately felt by all those around him.

> "He is a very proud man," [one of the characters says of Versilov] . . . and many of those who are very proud love to believe in God, especially those who despise people. It seems that many very strong people have some sort of natural craving to find someone or something to which they can bow down (*preklonitsya*). It is often difficult for the strong person to bear his strength." (I 3 VI)

Even the earlier voluptuaries Svidrigailov (*Crime and Punishment*) and Valkovsky (*The Insulted and the Injured*) are tinged with this dual nature.

Svidrigailov was in his wife's debt as a result of their earlier financial relations, and he speaks of himself as a "victim" in his love for her. (IV 1) He has also been thrashed for cheating at cards. (VI 3) Valkovsky tells the narrator of a former sadistic mistress. (III 10) Both men's debaucheries are sources of humiliation to them, much as Stavrogin's are to him. Self-humiliating aggressiveness is a feature of extreme sensuality in Dostoevsky.

Victimized characters bear strong *mana* in Dostoevsky's world; a victimized character who is himself an aggressor heightens the numinous aura which surrounds his person and his behavior. The key lies in Dostoevsky's view of the criminal himself as victim or "sufferer," mentioned both in *Notes from the House of the Dead* (II 4) and *The Diary of a Writer*:

> . . . The people say to the "unfortunates" as it were: "You have sinned and you suffer, but we have sinned also. Had we been in your place, we might have done worse. Had we been better ourselves, perhaps you would not be in prison. With the retribution for your crimes you have taken on the burden for everyone's lawlessness. Pray for us, and we will pray for you." (*The Diary of a Writer,* 1873, "The Environment.")

The criminal's punishment, then, is a substitutionary sacrifice for all men, and it produces a realization of communal guilt. A graphic example of such substitutionary punishment is the case of the house-painter Mikolka who confesses to Raskolnikov's crime out of a desire to take on his burden of suffering. An untranslatable pun suggests that he is a double or perhaps emanation of Raskolnikov. (Porfiry Petrovich says, "he is one of the schismatics" '*on iz raskolnikov*'.) Another example of this sort of substitution is found in the convicts who exchange sentences, often with similar motivations. (*Notes from the House of the Dead,* I 5) The criminal, by destroying another, destroys himself as well and places himself in that special category of vulnerable human beings alongside his victim. Herein lies the similarity of the other-destroying Raskolnikov and the self-destroying Sonya. "You have also had the strength to transgress (*perestupit,* 'step across')," he says to her. (*Crime and Punishment,* IV 4)

Criminals facing execution are symbolically important in *The Idiot* and they represent compellingly this combination of criminality and redemptive vulnerability. Early in the novel Myshkin describes three executions: to the footman he describes an execution he saw in France and to the Epanchin ladies he first describes the experiences of an acquaintance who was reprieved at the last moment and then outlines a picture of a criminal about to be guillotined for Adelaida to paint. In each case the approach of death gives the man an otherwordly quality which intensely fascinates the spectators and hearers. The moment of heightened consciousness immediately before death is stressed: "Then when you lay your head under the very knife and hear it sliding over your head, that quarter of a second is the most frightful of all." (I 2) "Those five minutes seemed to him an endless time. . . . Finally . . . he really began to wish that they would shoot him quickly." (I 5) "It is strange that people rarely faint in those vey last seconds. On the contrary, the mind is extraordinarily lively and must work at very high speed, like a machine wihch has been set in motion." (I 5) The same issues are important later in the description of Mme. Dubarry's execution.

Myshkin's fascination with such moments is implicitly linked with the ecstatic moments which introduce his seizures.

> The sensations of life, the consciousness of self was multiplied almost ten times at those moments which passed like lightning. The mind and heart were illuminated with an unusual light and it was as though all anxieties, doubts and disturbances were pacified at once. . . . But these moments . . . were still only the forewarning of that last second which initiated the seizure itself. That second was, of course, unbearable. (II 5)

The seizure, ending as it does in unconsciousness, is a death symbol, and Myshkin is a Christ figure. One more linkage is inescapable, then, a link with the one other executed criminal in the novel: the Christ of Rogozhin's Holbein painting. This painting is even mentioned, almost in the same breath, with the last execution description. Not only does the victimized criminal share the *mana* of vulnerability with other victimized characters; he is linked with the most important redeemer-figure in Dostoevsky's quasi-Christian system, the crucified Christ. The criminal, then, is seen as redeemer.

Sigmund Freud pointed this out in his essay on the Russian novelist:

> Dostoevsky's sympathy for the criminal . . . reminds us of the "holy awe" with which epileptics and lunatics were regarded in the past. A criminal to him is almost a Redeemer, who has taken on himself the guilt which must else have been borne by others. There is no longer any need to murder, since *he* has already murdered. . . ."[6]

This brings to light an important point. The aggressive Dostoevskian character, if he achieves salvation at all, always does so by working through his crime to the repentance which lies only beyond it. He never achieves salvation first and thereby avoids committing the crime. This is true most clearly for Raskolnikov, but it holds up even for Zosima if we consider the beating of his servant Afanasy, which occasions his repentance, as his crime. The drama of salvation in Dostoevsky always involves crime, not just original sin but specific personal crime, as an unavoidable step. Salvation for Dostoevsky's aggressive characters is always through crime. This is why many Christian thinkers are disturbed by Dostoevsky's works. Christian imagery and doctrine are used extensively, but the overall thrust of the work is heretical from a Christian point of view. The savior expiates the crime only by committing it.

Kirillov, in *The Devils*, enacts this expiatory drama in a special way, functioning both as redemptive victim and redemptive criminal in the same violent act. He believes that by premeditated and philosophically motivated suicide he will liberate mankind from the fear of death and initiate a new age. Willing to die for mankind, he is surrounded by Christ imagery. Witness the following dialogue:

> Krillov: "He who teaches that all are good will bring the world to an end."
> Stavrogin: "He who taught it was crucified."
> Krillov: "He will come, and his name is the man-god."
> Stavrogin: "The god-man?"
> Kirillov: "The man-god. That's the difference." (II 1 V)

Later Kirillov says, "I will begin and end, and will open the door. And I will save." (III 6 II)

For René Girard, Kirillov sees Christ as the revered and hated "Other" whom he imitates and corrects, making himself into a parody of Christ.[7] But he is a criminal savior, combining murderer and victim in a single self-destroying character. This Dostoevskian sacred drama is necessarily incomplete, however, since Kirillov's act leaves no possibility of repentance.

Tyrant and victim are locked in a peculiar symbiotic bond. Each needs the other; each must participate in the act of violent crime, by aggressing or submitting, in order to work through to his or her own special destiny or salvation. Violent crime is the sacrament of Dostoevsky's religion, and these two figures, the tyrant and the victim, are consecrated to it.

CHAPTER 9

PRIMAL MURDERS

The Brothers Karamazov, Dostoevsky's last and in many respects his most successful novel, resolves some of the moral issues presented earlier. The destructively perverse patterns of human relationships which characterized Dostoevsky's earlier fiction may be found here as well; relations between aggressive physical power and passive spiritual power form the axis upon which the novel turns. The symbol of the bow, used earlier, becomes even more central here. The building blocks are the same, but the novel as a whole rises to a new level as these relationships are transfigured by the inversion of the dominance hierarchy which occurs here.

What makes *The Brothers Karamazov* so unique? What force transfigures the power relationships between characters here, so destructive elsewhere? First the inversion of the dominance hierarchy which takes place here is a voluntary bow of master to servant, of strength to weakness, as is Raskolnikov's bow to Sonya in *Crime and Punishment*. This is symbolized by Father Zosima's bow to his servant Afanasy, a crucial image in the novel, as is bowing generally.

The novel's epigraph, ". . . Except a corn of wheat fall into the ground and die, it abideth alone, but if it die, it bringeth forth much fruit." (John 12:24) has meaning on several levels. It serves as the capstone to the system of religious imagery and meaning in this novel and in Dostoevsky's work as a whole. As such, it elucidates gestures such as Alyosha's bow to the earth, reflecting a sense of union with the universe and with God, or Zosima's bow to Dmitri, suggesting a veneration for expiatory suffering in a Christian context. With regard to the subject of the present study, the epigraph indicates that some sort of self-annihilation is as important here as it was in *The Double*. There its results were terrible, while here it is transfigured by the novel's system of religious meaning and becomes redemptive. The epigraph provides one of those luminous moments in which various systems of imagery and meaning intersect, illuminating both.

Another reason for the special status of this novel lies in the sacramental character of the deaths of Fyodor Karamazov, the paradigmatic tyrant, and Ilyusha Snegiryov, the paradigmatic victim. These "murders" re-enact in a ritual way the types of violence which can occur in Dostoevsky's world, and thus form a basis for personal conscience and social organization. "The Boys" and "The Russian Monk" sections of the novel, then, far from being peripheral or expendable as is often thought, are in fact central to the novel's mesage and to its unique status within Dostoevsky's work.

One of Dostoevsky's most important literary techniques is situation rhyme, the repetition of paradigmatic scenes to reinforce ideas, symbolic patterns or sets of relationships between characters. This technique of situation rhyme is especially crucial in *The Brothers Karamazov* and the most important recurrent paradigm is the dramatic bow. Dostoevsky had used such bows earlier in *Crime and Punishment* (Sonya to Raskolnikov, Raskolnikov to Sonya), *The Devils* (Marya Lebyadkina to Mme. Stavrogina), *A Raw Youth* (Dolgoruky's mother to Versilov) and even in the early novella *the Landlady* (Katerina to Murin). In *The Brothers Karamazov* the first such scene, Zosima's bow to Dmitry, forms the climax of the novel's first section. It is foreshadowed by a preoccupation with bowing etiquette as the guests arrive at the monk's cell. The narrator devotes much attention to the fact that old Karamazov and the members of his party do not make appropriate bows to Zosima, being put off by the elaborate bowing of the monks. (I 2 II) Only Dmitry makes a proper obeisance to Father Zosima upon entering. When Father Zosima returns this bow, going down on his knees before Dmitry, everyone is shocked and baffled. (II 2 III) The suggestion is made by some spectators that the elder is bowing down to suffering. This is reminiscent of *Crime and Punishment*, where that was the meaning of Sonya's bow to Raskolnikov.

But the real meaning of Zosima's bow lies in his own statements. He quotes his brother Markel thus: "there must be servants and masters, but let me be the servant of my servants, just as they are to me. And also, . . . every one of us has sinned greatly against all men, and I more than any." Once again these two ideas, power inversion and acceptance of personal guilt, are bound together as the center of the novel's moral system. Zosima's bow to Dmitry illustrates this; he achieves moral power through symbolic submission to aggressive physical power.

Bowing is also crucial in the balance of power between Katya and Dmitry.[1] When she comes to get the 4000 rubles from him, she is sacrificing her honor to save her father's, for the suggestion is unmistakable that the money is received in exchange for sexual favors. Katya is utterly in Dmitry's power and he savors the voluptuous delight of his domination. Yet her spiritual nobility subjugates him in a more lasting way.

> "At that moment she was beautiful because she was noble, while I was a scoundrel. . . . She was completely, completely at my mercy, body and soul. . . . That thought . . . so possessed my heart that it was almost drained by emotion. . . . I could scarcely breathe. . . . I looked at her for three seconds, for five, perhaps, with fearful hatred—that hate which is only a hair's breadth from love, from the maddest love." (I 3 IV)

They exchange bows: his represents mock respect while hers expresses the full extent of her submission and humiliation:

> "[I] bowed to her from the waist with a most respectful, a most impressive bow, believe me! She . . . suddenly bowed down, deeply and quietly, right at my feet—forehead on the floor—not a girls' boarding school bow, but a real Russian one [i.e., a complete prostration]." (I 3 IV)

Dmitry's response expresses the ambivalent attitude toward the self common to Dostoevskian characters in such situations, and it also suggests the erotic tensions involved in this inversion of the power balance, if the sword hanging at his belt is viewed as a phallic substitute: "I drew my sword and almost felt like stabbing myself right there . . . from ecstasy. Do you understand that one can kill oneself from ecstasy? But I didn't stab myself; I only kissed the sword and put it back in its sheath." (I 3 IV) The ecstatic combination of self-destructive and auto-erotic impulses is a typical Dostoevskian response to the voluptuous tension of this power struggle.

Katya's humble acceptance of Dmitry's sexual insult puts him in her power, just as surely as Sonya's submissive acceptance of sexual oppression gives her power over Raskolnikov in the earlier novel. Dmitry continues to identity himself as a bug, and to fail miserably in his attempts to live up to Katya's moral nobility. The message he sends to her through Alyosha expresses the reversal of their power roles. It is impossible to translate this nuance into good idiomatic English. Constance Garnett renders it as "He sends his compliments," but he actually says "[He] directed [me] to bow to you [for him]." (I 3 V) Thus the cycle of bowing is completed with this illustration of Dmitry's submission to Katya's moral superiority.

Raskolnikov and Sonya also exchange bows in *Crime and Punishment* and there also the act signifies an inversion in the dominance structure of their relationship. But there the stated purpose of the bows is to identify and venerate a sufferer. The same is said of Zosima's bow to Dmitry earlier in *The Brothers Karamazov*. This idea seems to work at cross purposes to the idea that the bow is directed toward the possessor of overt aggressive power. This contradiction is superficial, and in fact it makes clearer the connection between Raskolnikov and Dmitry. Both are aggressors who are about to take up a role as victim, as a result of their own violence. This apparent contradiction reinforces the idea of power reversal as the means to moral transformation in Dostoevsky's works.

Parallel to bowing, another act of apparent submission, kissing, also figures importantly in relationships involving personal dominance. Sometimes a kiss is used ingenuously as in Christ's kiss of the Grand Inquisitor and

Alyosha's parallel kiss of Ivan. Like Zosima's bow to Dmitry these kisses are dramatic climaxes which are left unexplained, and they are all the more dramatic for their ambiguity. In each case the character in a subordinate position, (a prisoner of the Inquisition, a younger and less experienced brother) replies to a rational and verbal attack by a silent kiss of loving acquiescence. And in each case, this act is more effective than a barrage of blows or arguments in overwhelming the opponent.

Elsewhere a kiss is withheld in a calculated and devastating way to get the better of an opponent. After Katya showers Grushenka's hand with kisses and thinks that she has extracted a promise that the latter will break with Dmitry, Grushenka makes it clear that she feels bound by no such promise and confirms her victory by withholding a kiss.

> "Do you know, angel lady, . . . I'm not going to kiss your hand after all. . . . That way you'll be left with the memory that you kissed my hand, but I didn't kiss yours. . . . I'll tell Mitya about it right away . . . and how he will laugh. . . ." (II 4 X)

Whether given or expressly withheld, whether ingenuous or calculated, these acts of apparent submission are among the most powerful weapons in the arsenal of Dostoevsky's competitive charcaters.

The relationship between Zosima and Alyosha presents the positive resolution of the pathology which has characterized friendships throughout Dostoevsky's work. The structure in which their relationship is cast is the monastic institution of elders, a hierarchical system which has all the features of dominance and submission noted in other Dostoevskian friendships:

> An elder—that is someone who takes your soul and your will into his soul and his will. Having chosen an elder, you suspend your own will and give it to him in complete obedience, with complete renunciation of self. He who subjects himself to this discipline does so voluntarily, in the hope of conquering himself, of mastering himself, of achieving . . . freedom . . . from his very self. . . ." (I 1 V)

The submission to an elder is an attempt to escape the self, just as surely as Golyadkin is trying to escape himself when he encounters his frightful double. Why are the results positive here? Zosima's ministrations with Alyosha are not directed toward strengthening his own domination but toward abetting Alyosha's self-discovery: "What are you talking about? Your place now is not here. I consecrate you for great service in the world. . . . But I don't doubt you; that is why I am sending you." (I 2 VIV) The stronger member of the relationships is interested in freeing his protege from his influence rather than in consolidating his control. The powerful individual voluntarily sacrifices his power in the interest of his weaker friend. The symbol for this is the idea of the master as servant of his servants, already quoted as part of Zosima's philosophy, derived from his brother Markel.

When Alyosha finds himself in a dominant position in a similar relationship with the younger Kolya Krasotkin, he behaves in much the same way. When Kolya says "I've come to learn from you, Karamazov," Alyosha replies, "And I from you." We are told that "Kolya was quite pleased with Alyosha. What struck him was that Alyosha dealt with him just as if he were 'completely grown up.'" (IV 10 IV) Later Alyosha says to his protege "Don't be like all the others, even if you're the only one who remains different, don't be like them . . . you will be a very unhappy person in your life . . . but nonetheless you will bless life on the whole." (IV 10 VI) The personal development of the disciple is the greatest concern of the master here, and he elevates the disciple to his own level for this purpose.[2] The relationship between Alyosha and Kolya echoes that between Zosima and Alyosha. This is another sort of situation rhyme in which it is not a paradigmatic scene but a paradigmatic relationship that finds a parallel elsewhere in the novel.

The key to this resolution of the problem of personal dominance lies in the story of Zosima's youth. In earlier works by Dostoevsky, meek self-abnegation was always associated with some form of weakness: with illness (epilepsy), masochism, or psychopathic alienation. The result of this pathological weakness was always destructive, no matter how beautiful and Christlike it may have seemed. In Father Zosima's moral system, self-abnegation must proceed from personal strength, not from congenital weakness, and the result of this sort of self-denial is positive. The duel Zosima almost fights illustrates this, for the young Zosima is no weakling but a reckless and debonair young officer possessed of all the advantages valued by his peers. He could easily have been a Silvio, a Pechorin, or Zverkov; in fact the circumstances of the duel are reminiscent of Pushkin's "The Shot." He discovers that a young woman to whom he has become attached is already engaged to an older, wealthier and higher ranking man:

> ". . . once in high society I had the chance to offend my 'opponent' for the most inconsequential of reasons. . . . He accepted my challenge, in spite of the tremendous difference between us (for I was younger than he was, insignificant and low-ranking), . . . out of a feeling of jealousy toward me." (II 6 IIc)

Preparing for the duel Zosima beats his servant Afanasy, behaving in typical Dostoevskian fashion. He is threatened by someone above him in the dominance hierarchy, and he responds by behaving sadistically toward someone beneath him in the same hierarchy. Upon arising to prepare for the duel and seeing the beauty of the morning, he is stricken with remorse for beating his servant, and it is this remorse which occasions his conversion. First he recalls Markel's idea that the master should be the servant of his servants, and concludes: "In truth, perhaps I am more than anyone else guilty before everyone, and even worse than all other men on earth!" (II 6 II c) Once again the ideas of power inversion and the acceptance of personal guilt are coupled and are the pivotal realizations in the character's transformation. At this moment Zosima "lay . . . face down on the bed, with his face pressed into the pillow. . . ." (II 6 II c), in exactly the same position as was the underground man before the last power reversal of *Notes from Underground*, but he takes the opposite path:

> "Afanasy," I said, "I struck you twice in the face yesterday. Forgive me," I said. He started just as though frightened. He looked at me and I could see that this would not be enough so I suddenly, just as I was, in my dress uniform, touched my forehead to the earth before his feet. "Forgive me," I said. (II 6 II c)

He returns to his friends calling himself a "conqueror" as a result of this act of submission.

Just as the bow to Afansy is the turning point in his conversion, so the ideal of power inversion becomes the cornerstone of his ethical system:

> It is impossible not to have servants in the world, but you should arrange things so that your servant will be freer in spirit in your presence than if he were not a servant. And why can I not be a servant to my servant. . . . This will serve as a foundation for the magnificent unification of mankind in the future, when men will not seek servants for themselves, when they will not desire to transform other people, like themselves, into their servants, as they now do, but on the contrary, will wish with all their strength to become the servant of all. . . ." (II 6 III f)

But the initiative belongs to the master; it is he who must become servant of his servant. The submission of the weak only exacerbates the imbalance of power; it is the person holding power who must surrender it. That is why Myshkin's Christlikeness is not sufficient, and that is why Zosima must be a Silvio before his conversion.

Just as the bond between Zosima and Alyosha resolves the pathology of Dostoevskian friendship, so the relationship between Dmitry and Grushenka presents a resolution of the pathology of love. Their relationship has all of the negative elements of the love of Rogozhin and Nastasya Filippova. Dmitry is just such a bully as Rogozhin, as is suggested by his treatment of Snegiryov and the servant Grigory. Even his physical portrait recalls Rogozhin:

> . . . a young man of 28, of medium height and pleasant features, . . . he was muscular, and showed signs of considerable physical strength. Nonetheless, his face had an unhealthy look. It was thin, his cheeks were sunken and gave off an unhealthy yellow color. His rather large, prominent, dark eyes had an expression of firm determination, and yet of vagueness as well. (II 2 VI) (See Chapter 5 for the description of Rogozhin.)

Grushenka toys with Dmitry's emotions, playing him off against her other lovers, just as Nastasya Filippova does with Rogozhin. Rogozhin was kept in the role of "footman" by his mistress, and Dmitry says something quite similar with regard to Grushenka:

> "I'll be her janitor. . . . I'll be her husband, it would be an honor. And when lovers come I'll go into the next room. I'll clean her friends' galoshes, heat up their samovar, run their errands." (I 3 V)

After the murder Grushenka expresses similar masochistic feelings, then rejects them as though wishing to reject that element in her character:

> "Now I will be your slave, your slave for my whole life! It is sweet to be a slave! . . . Kiss me, beat me, torment me, do what you will with me. . . . Stop, wait, later, I don't want it to be that way . . ." she suddenly pushed him away. (III 8 VIII)

Both reject the self-destructive sides of their characters and, perhaps because of their mutual willingness to sacrifice for each other, they are finally able to neutralize the destructive effects of the sadomasochistic tangle in which they find themselves at the begining of the novel.

What is it that effects these changes? What changes Alyosha from a novice under the control of his elder into a leader capable of instructing those younger than himself; what changes Dmitry from a brawling bully under the thumb of a capricious woman into a man ready to take on adult responsibilities? Unquestionably, it is the murder of their tyrannical father. Both brothers, and to a lesser extent Ivan as well, undergo emotional experiences, *during the very hours that their father is being murdered* by their half-brother Smerdyakov, which changes them from boys into men.[3] The simultaneity of these experiences with the murder is obscured by the sprawling character of the novel, but may be easily discovered by attention to chronology. These experiences involve the acceptance of personal guilt by each brother, an idea which, as we have already seen, is the crux of Dostoevsky's moral and esthetic system.

This idea is also crucial in Freud's anthropological treatise *Totem and Taboo,* where it is seen as a direct outgrowth of the cooperative murder of a tyrannical father by a group of brothers, and where it is also instrumental in the transition to adulthood for those brothers. In fact, Freud's anthropological hypothesis in this book, written thirty-five years after Dostoevsky's death, is closely parallel to the events described in *The Brothers Karamazov.*[4] Freud is seeking an explanation of the transition in human evolution from the patriarchal kinship groups of certain hominid primates to the fraternally organized tribes of primitive society. Several primate societies are autocratic, and the strongest male in the group has absolute control of the younger males, his sons, and unquestioned sexual rights to the group's females, his wives and daughters. Trying to explain the transition from this society to a fraternal tribe with complex religious rituals, Freud hypothesizes that at some point the sons must have risen up against the father, murdered him, and taken over the tribe. Acceptance of communal guilt for this act establishes the social order of the tribe, its morality and its religion. The murdered father becomes an ancestral deity, more powerful in death than in life.

> After they had got rid of him, . . . a sense of guilt made its appearance. . . . The dead father became stronger than the living one had been—for . . . what had up to then been prevented by his actual existence was thenceforward prohibited by the sons themselves . . . ("deferred obedience"). . . . They revoked their deed by forbidding the killing of the totem, the substitute for their father; and they renounced its fruits by resigning their claim to the women who had now been set free. They thus created out of their fundamental sense of guilt the two fundamental taboos of totemism. . . .[5]

The taboos he had established, proscribing sexual intercourse with the women of the tribe and prohibiting any challenge to his own authority, became the fundamental prohibitions of the society, the incest taboo and the taboo against killing the totem animal, which represents the murdered ancestor. The basic religious ritual is the sacrificial meal in which the totem animal is killed and eaten, reenacting the primal murder. Thus the communal guilt felt by the brothers who have murdered their father forms the cornerstone of social behavior. (In bad repute for many years, Freud's anthropological hypothesis is currently being reevaluated more positively by several anthropologists.[6] In any case the similarity with Dostoevsky is significant.)

This situation is really quite closely parallel to the situation in *The Brothers Karamazov.*[7] There are two totemic murders in this novel, one of the tyrannical patariarch, Fyodor Karamazov, and the other of a victimized child, Ilyusha Snegiryov. As has already been demonstrated, the victim has totemic power in Dostoevsky's work generally, and by examining the two parallel murders in this novel we may come to understand more fully the movement from the murder of the tyrannical patriarch to its representation by its opposite, the murder of a powerless innocent.

One of the striking things about Dostoevsky's early and middle work generally is the absence of father figures. Older men in these novels are usually lecherous suitors of the young heroines, but they are seldom the fathers of any major characters. (Partial exceptions are *Poor Folk, Netochka Nezvanova* and *Crime and Punishment*, where the father is a weak-willed drunkard, absent much of the time, and *The Insulted and the Injured,* where the father is dissolute and tyrannical, in some respects a forerunner of Fyodor Pavlovich Karamazov.) The family is always incomplete or damaged. The issue of adolescent rebellion against parental authority is crucial to personal identity in the last two novels,[8] and yet this central issue is avoided earlier. It is significant that Dostoevsky resolves the issues of dominance and personal identity, so prevalent in his works, only when he faces head on the issue of adolescent rebellion against parental authority.

The most significant treatment of a father/son relationship prior to *The Brothers Karamazov* is found in *A Raw Youth*, written in 1875, just before *The Brothers Karamazov*. Many similar details suggest that the former was a preliminary study for the latter: both novels present a mimetic or Oedipal triangle in which father and son compete for the same woman. The treatment of this triangle in *A Raw Youth* is much more reminiscent of Dostoevsky's earlier work, however. There is a strong admixture of adoration in Dolgoruky's attitude toward Versilov, counterbalancing the hostility. This adoring attitude is totally absent from *The Brothers Karamazov*. The novels share the element of a second, spiritual father figure (Makar Dolgoruky, Father Zosima) contrasting with the dissolute physical father. The central issue of rebellion against parental authority is not resolved in *A Raw Youth* and the novel flounders as a result.

In *The Brothers Karamazov*, where these issues are resolved, the idea of parental tyranny is echoed on several levels. The Karamazov household represents a situation in which the father limits the actions of all four sons, arouses hatred from each of them (except Alyosha), and even competes with the eldest for the sexual attentions of a woman. This situation is echoed even more graphically by the Samsonov household, where Dmitry tries to scare up some money at his moment of need. Even Samsonov's house symbolizes the structure of his family:

This house . . . had two stories, with outbuildings in the yard and with an added wing. On the first floor lived Samsonov's two married sons with their families, an elderly sister and one unmarried daughter. In the wing were situated his two stewards, one of whom also had a large family. His children and his stewards were crowded into their quarters, but the old man had the whole second floor to himself and wouldn't let even his daughter live up there. . . . They all trembled before their father. (III 8 I)

Needing money in the struggle with his own tyrannical father, Dmitry applies for help to another tyrannical father who refuses him, clearly as a stand-in for his own father. Samsonov is inordinately outraged by Dmitry's request, and makes threats which frighten even his own strapping son, and finally falls ill from overexcitement. All of this echoes what is going on in Dmitry's struggle with his real father.

Later that same night, the night his father is murdered by his half brother Smerdyakov, Dmitry undergoes changes which signify his rite of passage into adulthood. Early in the evening his behavior is called childlike by the narrator (III 8 V), and his peasant driver Andrei calls him a "little child." (III 8 VI) His transformation is accompanied by several symbols of crossing over into a new reality. Madame Khokhlakova, in a crucially placed comic relief scene, misunderstands his request for money and tells him to go to the gold mines to make his fortune, and she gives him a cross to consecrate him to his "new life." (III 8 III) Just after he almost attacks his father, he climbs over a fence, and in doing so he is forced to attack his surrogate father, Grigory, who tries to restrain him. The following morning he plans to cross another boundary, to kill himself: "Tomorrow at dawn, when 'the sun ascends,' Mitya will leap over that fence. . . ." (III 8 V) In his own thinking these hours of his passage to maturity are the last of his life; his actions are seen as preparation for self-destruction, not self-renewal. Finally he is required to strip naked, something he finds intensely humiliating and which fills him with self-loathing. He must put on the clothes of another man, another clear symbol of the transformation of his personal identity. He puts on the clothes of Kalganov, a twenty-year old youth who is even closer than he is to the borderline between adolescence and manhood. (III 9 VI)

The experience which brings about Mitya's final change is his dream of the weeping child, and the steps in this transformation are familiar to us from "The Dream of a Ridiculous Man" and other works. He feels pity for the child in the dream and immediately after this he is able to accept his personal guilt for the events of the previous night. (III 9 VIII) A comparison of his statements about the murder before and after the dream illustrates this. Before the dream he says: "I am not guilty of that blood . . . I wanted to kill him, but I am not guilty! Not I!" (III 9 III) After the dream he still insists that he did not strike the blow that felled his father, but he admits his guilt for desiring the death and accepts his punishment for it.

> Good people, we are all cruel, we are all monsters, we all cause people to weep, mothers and children at the breast. But of all, let it be settled here and now, I am the basest reptile of all. . . . I am not guilty of my father's blood! I accept my punishment, not because I killed him, but because I wanted to kill him, and perhaps really would have killed him. . . . (III 9 IX)

Just as in other works by Dostoevsky, pity for a suffering innocent occasions a realization and acceptance of shared personal guilt. And just as in Freud's reconstruction of anthropological pre-history, acceptance of personal guilt in the murder of one's father brings about an acceptance of mature social responsibility.

During the night of his father's murder, Ivan also experiences feelings of transformation and of personal guilt. He is on the train to Moscow all that night, and he thinks:

> "Away with all the past. I'm done with the old world forever, and may I have no news, no echo, from it. To a new life, new places, and no looking back!" But instead of delight his soul filled with such gloom, and his heart ached with such anguish, as he had never known in his life before. He was thinking all night. The train flew on, and only at daybreak, when he was approaching Moscow, he suddenly roused himself "I am a scoundrel," he whispered to himself. (II 5 VII)

Of all the four brothers, Ivan is the one least willing to admit his guilt for the murder, so although his meditations on the night of the murder follow the same pattern as do those of his brothers, his complete acceptance of his own culpability does not come until much later in the novel, after Smerdyakov's confession. Here, however, his response to this realization follows exactly the pattern noted in "The Dream of a Ridiculous Man." On his way to the third interview with Smerdyakov he callously pushes a drunken peasant into a snowdrift. The man will surely freeze to death if unattended. After Smerdyakov's confession, which clearly implicates Ivan in the murder, Ivan spends considerable time and effort getting the man safely to the police station. (IV 11 VIII) Compare this with the ridiculous man's response to the starving orphan girl before and after his dream. The situation rhyme is striking.

Alyosha is the one brother who is in no way guilty of complicity in his father's death, and yet even his thoughts on that night follow the pattern of of acceptance of guilt! "He wanted to forgive everyone for everything and to ask forgiveness, oh, not for himself, but for everyone and everything, and 'on my behalf others are asking for forgiveness too.'" (III 7 IV) A desire to ask forgiveness for a vague sense of guilt is combined here with a sense of community with all men, as was the case with Dmitry. (III 9 IX) He has these feelings as his physical father is being murdered by his half brother, but also just one day after the death of his spiritual father. In fact, the immediate occasion for these feelings is his presence by the coffin of this spiritual father, who has been humiliated in the eyes of many of the townspeople. Freud maintains that the dead father is resurrected in the social and individual superego, as his prohibitions and precepts become the chief religious and social taboos in the social group and in the individual personality. The superego becomes the representative of the deposed father in the adult personality or in the fraternal society. Something very like this happens to Alyosha:

> It was as though a certain idea seized the sovereignty of his mind, to remain there all his life, for ever and ever. He fell on the earth a weak youth, but he rose up a resolute champion . . . "Someone visited my soul at that hour," he said. . . . (III 7 IV)

The "visitor" which enters his soul and makes him a man is the combined image of his physical and spiritual fathers, both of whom are being in some way or other laid to rest in these moments.

A situation rhyme which connects Alyosha with Dmitry in this rite of passage is the repeated reference to the younger brother's climbing of fences. When he meets with Dmitry the first time he takes a short cut, jumping over many fences. Dmitry helps him over the last one, and he leaps it "with the agility of a barefoot street urchin." (I 3 III) The next day he climbs over the same fence again, this time without Dmitry's help. (II 5 II) The frequent references to fence climbing by both of these brothers underscores the changes they are experiencing. Climbing over fences is important for other characters as well, and not only in this novel. Dmitry is astride a fence when he strikes and nearly kills Grigory, and just after he has come close to killing his father. This is, of course, the crucial moment in his own rite of passage. The image is used in *A Raw Youth* as well, but significantly, young Arkady does *not* succeed in getting across the fence in that novel, suggesting that his transformation is incomplete. Other sorts of boundaries are related to this image: the underground man is obsessed with the boundary presented by a wall, but characteristically, he does not cross the boundary but smashes himself against it; Raskolnikov's crime is seen as the crossing of a boundary, suggesting once again that his crime signifies a rite of passage, both before the fact in his own eyes, and also, in a very different way, in the overall religious context of the novel. Perhaps this connection between the boundary and a crime elucidates the use of the image with Stinking Lizaveta. She climbs a fence just before giving birth to Smerdyakov, an event which reveals the crime which had been perpetrated against her. This is also immediately followed by her death, which links her with Dmitry, who speaks of his planned suicide as the crossing of a boundary. The image has several related meanings, but in *The Brothers Karamazov* the dominant one is the idea of rite of passage, that is, of sudden personal crisis and consequent maturation.

So all three of the brothers (Smerdyakov is not taken as seriously) experience a rite of passage during the night of their father's murder. This transformation involves the characteristic Dostoevskian steps of compassion, guilt, and finally achievement of adult identity and relations with others. The guilt is connected with the murder of their father, and the maturity is achieved (in at least one case) through an assimilation of a paternal figure as superego.

But another death in *The Brothers Karamazov* also functions as a totemic murder. Ilyusha Snegiryov is an outcast from the society of his fellows. (His relations with the other boys in the town recall the school experiences of the boy who was to become the underground man.[9]) Ilyusha's row with his young friends appears to bring on the consumptive attack that finally kills him. When Alyosha suggests "[The fights] are very dangerous; they might kill him; they're stupid children; a stone might fly and break a head," Ilyusha's father replies, "Yes, it's already happened, sir, not in the head but in the chest, above the heart. Today he got hit with a stone—there's a bruise. He came home crying and groaning and now he's fallen ill." (IV 4 VII) Of course, Dmitry's insult to Snegiryov is an equally important cause of Ilyusha's emotional disturbance; this links him with the criminal aggression of the central plot of the novel as well. But it is the taunting by his school friends that exacerbates this insult and makes it intolerable. In the rough drafts they commit even worse crimes, such as theft and the torture of a four-year-old boy.[10] When the boys finally realize what they have done and befriend Ilyusha, it is too late, and Kolya Krasotkin's attempt to help by his surprise gift only hastens Ilyusha's death: "If Krasotkin, who suspected nothing had only know how disastrously and fatally [*ubiistvenno*] that moment might affect the child's health, nothing could have induced him to play the trick he played." (IV 10 V) This little "fraternity" of schoolboys really does kill Ilyusha. The fact that his corpse does not smell of decay (Epilogue III) underlines the sacral character of his death, especially after the whole brouhaha over the unpleasant smelling decomposition of Zosima's supposedly sanctified body.

In this context it becomes clear that Alyosha's speech at the stone, often treated as a misplaced loose thread, or as only groundwork for a sequel, is in fact integral, both to this novel and in Dostoevsky's work as a whole. In this speech, Alyosha makes clear the totemic nature of the "murder" of Ilyusha:

> Let us agree right here at Ilyusha's stone that we wil never forget, first of all, Ilyusha, and second, each other. And no matter what happens to us later in life, even if we don't see each other for twenty years, let us remember how we buried the poor boy at whom we used to throw stones (remember, there at the bridge?), and how afterwards we all grew so fond of him. . . . Don't ever forget how good it has been here for all of us together, united by a good and kind feeling which has made us, while we loved that poor boy, perhaps better than we really are. . . . No matter how evil we may become (God forbid!), when we remember how we buried Ilyusha, how we loved him in the last days, and how we talked together like friends right here at this stone, then even the most cruel and mocking one among us, if we become like that, will still not dare laugh, even inwardly, at his former kindness and goodness in this moment! What's more, perhaps this very recollection will be enough to restrain him from a great evil. . . . Well then, who has united us in this good and kind feeling which we will remember from now on and will set our minds to remember forever, all our lives?—who but Ilyusha, the good boy, the kind boy, the boy who is dear to us for ever and ever! We will never forget him, eternal and blessed memoery be to him in our hearts, from this time forth and even for evermore! (Epilogue III)

The biblical language is not mere rhetoric here, for Alyosha is laying the groundwork for a religious myth which will act as a basis for social interaction.[11] He is not forgetting Ilyusha's spiteful and sadistic behavior with the boys and with Zhuchka when he extolls Ilyusha's kindness and goodness, although he may hope the boys will forget. He is establishing a social superego based on mutual guilt for the killing of Ilyusha.[12] It is this guilt which lays the groundwork for social interaction and religious morality, just as in the aftermath of the totemic murder described by Freud in *Totem and Taboo*.

So there are two totemic murders in *The Brothers Karamazov*, inversely parallel to each other: the murder of the tyrannical father by his sons, and an opposite situation, the death of a weakling schoolboy at the hands of his stronger schoolmates. As has been illustrated in the previous chapters, it is the second of these characters that functions as a totemic creature in Dostoevsky's works, having special taboos against its destruction, and emerging with mysterious powers. Yet it is the first of these murders that accords with the anthropological prehistory later hypothesized by Freud.

René Girard does not mention *The Brothers Karamazov* in his ethnological study of sacrifice, *Violence and the Sacred,* but his analysis there provides a useful framework for understanding this transfer of ritual violence from tyrant to victim. He rejects Freud's idea of communal murder in hominid behavioral evolution. According to Girard that murder was not of a patriarch but of a surrogate victim. This is necessary, he says in order to deflect the cycle of violence rather than perpetuate it. The situation in *The Brothers Karamazov* demonstrates this principle so well that one wonders why Girard fails to mention it, especially in view of his perceptive writings on Dostoevsky elsewhere. Both murders take place in Dostoevsky's novel, but it is the murder of the surrogate victim, rather than that of the tyrant, which is surrounded with explicit ritual significance.[13] Girard does mention elsewhere that the primordial crime in Dostoevsky is not patricide but infanticide.[14]

In the context of Dostoevsky's novels, this transference of ritual violence from tyrant to victim is a response to the rigidly structured dominance hierarchy in which rank is an important principle of organization. Aggression directed upward on this autocratic hierarchy is prohibited. Faced with the impossibility of meaningful challenge to authority, Dostoevsky's characters often direct their hostilities against those below them in the hierarchy (or against themselves). Again and again we have seen Dostoevsky's pathological heroes behavior masochistically with their superiors and sadistically with their inferiors. The two totemic murders of *The Brothers Karamazov,* then, illustrate the two directions aggression may take in such a hierarchy. Aggression upward, illustrated by the murder of the old man, is the basic impulse, but this impulse is absolutely frustrated, and hence effectively repressed. Aggression downward on the hierarchy, illustrated by the killing of Ilyusha, is the result of this frustration; the low-ranking figure is the butt of transferred hostilities which the aggressor would like to direct against his superiors. As a result, downward-directed aggression is a more common event, and thus a more serious threat to the social fabric. It must be taken seriously in Dostoevsky's moral system and prohibited in the strongest possible terms. The totemic features of vulnerability and weakness in Dostoevsky's works represent the writer's attempt to deal with the sadistic behavior resulting from the frustrations of the rigidly structured hierarchy of his novels.[15] The special status of victimized characters both protects them and makes possible a moral challenge to authority which would otherwise be impossible in such an environment.

The two ritual murders of *The Brothers Karamazov* dramatize the two possibilities for aggressive action in a sacramental way. The repressed upward-directed aggression and the frustration reaction of downward-directed aggression are both effectively prohibited by the primal murders of the prototypical tyrant Fyodor Karamazov and the prototypical victim Ilyusha Snegiryov.

CHAPTER 10

THE DOMINANCE HIERARCHY
IN POLITICAL BEHAVIOR[1]

How do Dostoevsky's non-fictional writings fit into the picture outlined above for his novels? Generally speaking, his journalism is lackluster viewed alongside his fictional spellbinders, and he spent a great deal of time beating the drum for jingoistic and reactionary causes such as pan-Slavism and the Balkan wars. One point of contact between the journalism and the fiction, however, is the continuing reliance on the idea of unredeemed society as a competitive dominance hierarchy and his insistence that self-renunciation is the only way to resolve the problems of such a society. As in much of the fiction (particularly *The Brothers Karamazov*) these power relationships and reversals are often symbolized by the image of the dramatic bow or obeisance.

Dostoevsky maintained that the need for self-assertion was a basic law of nature (using one of the buzz-words of the utilitarian nihilists to emphasize his anti-utilitarian point). Society has a need to recognize and bow down to the exceptional person, he argued, (interestingly, he included both the self-abnegating *yurodivy* and the despotic patriarch of old believer society in this category), but he felt that this need for self-assertion had reached a pathological state.[2] Contemporary European society, he maintained in *Winter Notes on Summer Impressions* (1863), his account of a trip to Western Europe, was based on a radical assertion of the rights of the isolated individual at the expense of others. (VI) This view of society is recapitulated in Raskolnikov's dream in the epilogue of *Crime and Punishment* (Epilogue, 2), where this "infectious" atomism causes wars to break out. The same view is expounded by Zosima's nocturnal visitor (*The Brothers Karamazov*, VI, 2, d), a repentant murderer (cf. Raskolnikov) who intends to confess and who is important in Zosima's spiritual development:

> For nowadays everyone strives to separate himself to the highest possible degree, each wants to experience the fullness of life in himself, but instead, the result of all his efforts is only complete self destruction (lit. "suicide") rather than the fullness of life, for instead of the complete affirmation of his own being, each falls into complete isolation. . . . Each gathers wealth in his own isolation, and thinks: 'How strong I am now and how secure,' and he does not realize, the fool, that the more he gathers the more he sinks into his suicidal impotence.

Dostoevsky saw modern society as the product of the dissolution of an earlier patriarchal society. It could only be redeemed, he thought, by each individual's surrender of his prerogatives to the group. This bow of the individual to the masses would produce a fraternal mode of society organization in the future, as long as the bow was mutual and society restored the prerogatives thus sacrifed (*Winter Notes* VI).[3] This of course is precisely the stumbling block in a society like Russia's, based, as Dostoevsky so aptly noted, on the tyranny of the strong over the weak.

More concretely, Dostoevsky's view of the relations between the Russian nobility and peasantry illustrates his concept of the dominance hierarchy on the level of group interaction. The Russian aristocracy, according to Dostoevsky, had been guilty of "an irrational slavish submission . . . to the European forms of culture," but had lorded it over the people. (*Winter Notes*, III).[4] The situation is that of the classic Dostoevskian sado-masochistic hierarchy, reminding us of the underground man, who responds to his ill treatment at the hands of his old school buddies by emotionally bludgeoning an impressionable prostitute who falls into his clutches. Elsewhere Dostoevsky made the same pattern explicit on an international plane when he suggested the Russian colonization of Asia as a means of developing a sense of national identity. The Russians' status as "Europeans" would make them masters in Asia, while their "Asian" status had made them slaves in Europe (*The Diary of a Writer*, Jan., 1881, II, 4). In fact the journalistic writings are peppered with comments which provide fine illustrations of mimetic desire in the international arena, as Geoffrey Kabat has observed. Here Dostoevsky speaks of Russia's offended solitude in the European community ("Apropos of the Exhibition") and its attempts to imitate Western Europe and become a great European power ("Daydreams and Fantasies"). He even uses his favorite image of the bow to describe the relationship of Russia to the West ("On Lying").

For Dostoevsky, then, the relationship between the aristocracy and the masses, like that between Russia and the West, was characterized by a power imbalance similar to those of his novels. The aristocracy had tyrannized over the people even as it had slavishly capitulated to Western Europe. What should the aristocratic Russian do to correct this situation, in Dostoevsky's opinion? He should bow to the people, sacrificing his extraordinary power of privilege to the general welfare. ("A Series of Articles on Russian Literature," I, 5) Lev Shestov saw Dostoevsky's entire late career as an obeisance to the people, particularly to its criminal element, as depicted in *Notes from the House of the Dead*.[5] Nikolai Berdyaev, Shestov's contemporary, noted that for Dostoevsky, as for the Slavophiles, the peasantry represented a mysterious force opposed to the self, the "not–I" before which the intelligentsia felt guilt and to which it must bow.[6] These thinkers realized that strength bowing to weakness is a central image in Dostoevsky's sociological writings, just as it is aesthetically central in *The Brothers Karamazov*.

Several of Dostoevsky's characters present visions of society in which dominance of the weak by the strong plays a central role. In *Crime and Punishment* Raskolnikov and the police official Porfiry Petrovich discuss an article on crime which the former had written several months before murdering the old pawnbroker. In this article Raskolnikov had maintained that humanity may be divided into two groups: the weak and unreflective masses and a strong controlling minority. The latter group directs the destiny of the former and may use any means, moral or immoral, to achieve the welfare of the masses. (II 5) Actually this vision of society reflects actual conditions in Russia during the nineteenth century, where a tiny elite ruled the masses. (Structurally, it also describes the situation in the current century, although the identity of the elite has changed.) Raskolnikov is shown to be incorrect, not in his depiction of Russian society, but in his view that the strong elite may disregard moral considerations. In the course of the novel Raskolnikov discovers that only by bowing to the meek and downtrodden (Sonya) and identifying with his own pitiful victim (Lizaveta) can he be regenerated. The question of regeneration of society, Porfiry Petrovich's "New Jerusalem" is left unresolved in this novel. Raskolnikov's dream in the epilogue leaves us with a vision of a society in radical dissolution, with the disease of violence running rampant.

An account of social organization similar to Raskolnikov's article on crime is held up to ridicule in *The Devils* when the revolutionary theorist Shigalyov propounds his doctrines. Poor Shigalyov has followed the logic of absolute freedom to its necessary conclusion and has arrived at unlimited despotism, but he assures his friends that no other solution is possible. (II 7 II) Although it claims to be a vision of the future, Shigalyov's utopia, in which ten percent of the population enslaves the other ninety percent, reflects the situation in tsarist Russia (and, mutatis mutandis, in the Soviet Union). On the whole, *The Devils* offers even less hope than does *Crime and Punishment* for the redemption of such a society. Pyotr Verkhovensky, the unrepentant rabble-rouser of that novel, accepts Shigalyov's sociological views wholeheartedly, if somewhat cynically, adding only the idea of Stavrogin as a figurehead, "with the aura of a victim," to give the masses someone to worship. (II 8)

The last of Dostoevsky's misguided utopians is Ivan Karamazov. In his "Legend of the Grand Inquisitor" (II 5 V) (which is foreshadowed by his article on church courts, I 2 V), we see most clearly the pathos of the tyrant which was implicit in the utopias of Raskolnikov and Shigalyov. The inquisitor is a truly benevolent man who sincerely desires the best for his pitiful subjects. They in turn long to be subjugated and want nothing more than material comforts and an object of worship. Furthermore, the Christ of the inquisitor legend is not the *New Testament's* Christ, but simply the opponent of the inquisitor's utopia. In fact, in his defense of a freedom which causes suffering, his ideas resemble those of the underground man. The inquisitor's case is presented so attractively that some thinkers, such as D. H. Lawrence, have seen him as the victor in the polemic with Christ.[7] Others have agreed that Dostoevsky answers the objections of Ivan's inquisitor only with difficulty.

But the inquisitor's kingdom is not really a misguided vision of utopia, but Dostoevsky's view of human society in its natural state. In unredeemed society, according to the inquisitor legend, the masses yearn to be subjugated. The ruler obliges them through a brutal policy of executions and then offers them a god who is none other than the victim (Christ) whom he is willing to execute once again. Christ, with his gentle kiss of acquiescence, threatens to upset this power balance. This kiss is parallel to the many bows of the novel, but not identical with them. It does not represent submission to the inquisitor's social views, but ignores them and suggests personal acceptance and forgiveness of the inquisitor himself. Thus it places Christ on a higher moral plane. This inverts, and potentially redeems, the power structure.

CHAPTER 11

THE STRUCTURE OF DOSTOEVSKY'S IMAGES

It would seem appropriate, by way of conclusion, to outline the grand overarching system of which each piece of Dostoevsky's writing forms a part. Indeed, that is the purpose of a critical work such as this one, to outline the structure of ideas and images which forms the framework of Dostoevsky's entire literary output. Should it not be possible to construct a "morphology of the Dostoevskian novel," a set of formulas, however complex, which applies to each of the works?

The structures used by Dostoevsky are not amenable to such systematic finality, for two reasons. First the structure which underlies these novels is a loose thematic or ideological one, and second, the structure is assembled from the ground up, through the connections and similarities of the individual building blocks, rather than being imposed by a skeletal superstructure. The principle of formal unity here is repetition with variation, doubling of many different kinds, situation rhyme. We can identify paradigms and observe parallel contours in Dostoevsky's novels, but we can never produce a neat formula which will explain the whole. To return to the anthropological metaphor which has informed much of this study, it would be possible to produce a theme index to Dostoevsky's works, but a "morphology" in the manner of Propp would not be feasible. The repetition of paradigms constantly gives the impression that such a morphology could be constructed, but there are too many variables to allow such neat formulas.

Using the dominance hierarchy as a key, this study has outlined one important set of recurring images in Dostoevsky's works, the tyrant-victim paradigm. The closest we can come to a formula uniting these images is to state the general principle that aggression in Dostoevsky tends to produce an inversion in the dominance hierarchy. The aggressor takes on the vulnerability of his victim, often with redemptive results. The permutations of this paradigm, outlined above, are too complex to be further formulized. We can, however, begin to catalog the parallel contours of the various images and themes relating to the paradigm. The metaphors used earlier (the jigsaw puzzle in Chapter 1, the building in the previous paragraph) are only partially appropriate, a better metaphor is that of a kaleidoscope.[1] The individual bits of imagery or ideology retain their shape, but each twist of the kaleidoscope rearranges them in new configurations. Furthermore, looking in the wrong end of the tube, without the proper illumination, one sees only a disorganized pile of stones. The technique of doubling or situation rhyme is kaleidoscopic. Again and again as we read Dostoevsky's novels, we have a sense of *déjà lu*,[2] we recognize elements we have seen before, arranged in new ways. It is these repetitions that form the unifying web in Dostoevsky's works.

The repetition may involve characters, relationships, scenes and details. Character doubling has received the most attention. Major characters (Raskolnikov, Stavrogin) are often surrounded by others who echo a single personality trait, giving the reader the sense that the character is surrounded by shadows or reflections. These character doublings form a structural principle in novels like *Crime and Punishment* or *The Devils*. In contrastive doubling, opposition rather than repetition becomes a structural principle (*The Idiot, The Eternal Husband*). Doubling operates across the boundaries of the novels as well. Parfyon Rogozhin and Dmitry Karamazov, Father Zosima and Tikhon (*The Devils*), Svidrigailov and Valkovsky (*The Insulted and the Injured*) are doubles who appear in different novels. The web is seamless, and in a sense all of Dostoevsky's works may be said to form a single work of art, a meta-novel, if you will, with reverberations rumbling from one novel into another.

Even the rough drafts may be included in this seamless web. For instance, the "idiot" of the early drafts of that novel never appears in the finished product, but is clearly a double of Stavrogin and Versilov in later novels. To return to the kaleidoscope metaphor, the rough drafts appear as configurations not quite yet in focus, but with the recognizable Dostoevskian elements present. For example, in *The Devils* Shatov slaps Stavrogin, but in the drafts it is Stavrogin who slaps Shatov. The slap is present from an early stage, and Stavrogin's behavior, in either case, is seen as a spiritual feat (*podvig*), a part of his burden. The process of finding the final form for the familiar paradigm is a matter of fine focusing for Dostoevsky.

It is not only characters that are doubled, but relationships between characters. The bond between Alyosha and Zosima is echoed by that between Kolya Krasotkin and Alyosha; the relationship between Rogozhin and Myshkin is echoed by that between Rogozhin and Ippolit in the same novel and by Velchaninov and Trusotsky in *The Eternal Husband*. The numerous relationships between older men and younger women provide another instance of doubling of relationships.

Scenes are doubled as well, particularly bows, slaps and, more broadly speaking, inversions of the dominance hierarchy. Other examples of scene doubling include execution in *The Idiot,* beatings and scenes of sexual oppression in *Crime and Punishment*, and, across novel boundaries, the deaths of Swiss Marie in *The Idiot* and Ilyusha Snegiryov in *The Brothers Karamazov*, the torture of animals in *White Nights, Notes from Underground* and *The Brothers Karamazov*, and fence climbing in *A Raw Youth* and *The Brothers Karamazov*. A variant of scene doubling is the doubling of ideological structures, as in the three utopian articles by Raskolnikov, Shigalyov and Ivan Karamazov.

Occasionally doubling will move in two of these directions at once. For instance, the relationship between Rogozhin and his adolescent admirer Ippolit doubles that between the former and Prince Myshkin, but the scene in which Rogozhin visits Ippolit (III 6) parallels Svidrigailov's visit to Raskolnikov in *Crime and Punishment* (IV 1). Both enter unnoticed in the dark of night, interrupting a dream (or daydream), and both seem to be a continuation of that dream. The form of the doubling (the identical scene) may be distinguished from the content of the doubling (parallel doubling underlining Raskolnikov's criminal side in the one case, and contrastive doubling embodying Ippolit's adolescent dreams in the other). Another example of this distinction may be found in Father Zosima's midnight visitor. Ideologically, he echoes some of Kirillov's ideas, others of Raskolnikov, but in form, his visits parallel those of Ivan's imaginary devil.

Finally, on the simplest level, there is doubling of details. Examples are doors locked from the inside in *Crime and Punishment*,[3] spider and insect imagery throughout the works,[4] involvement with Skoptsy in *The Idiot* (Rogozhin) and the rough drafts for *The Devils* (Stavrogin), and epilepsy in *The Idiot* (Myshkin) and *The Brothers Karamazov* (Smerdyakov).

The structure of Dostoevsky's novels is a constantly shifting pattern of parallel contours, usually thematic and ideological rather than formal. This system cannot be fully catalogued since the patterns are continually merging into one another, shifting in and out of focus, changing meaning and even shape, before our eyes. They cannot be fully mapped anymore than can the mind of the novelist. All we can do is identify the most salient themes and point out the ways in which they are usually embodied in the thematic structure of the novels, drafts and expository writings.

The set of themes relating to the dominance hierarchy certainly lies close to the core of Dostoevsky's mentality, and the inversion of the dominance hierarchy through the moral power of the victimized character forms a structural core for many of his most important works.

The tyrant-victim paradigm is not the only system of related images in Dostoevsky's work. Finally, we must place this configuration of themes in perspective by examining its relation to the other, similar, configurations important in Dostoevsky's work, including, but not limited to, religious, historical-biographical, psychological, social and familial systems of image-ry. These headings are focal points of thematic interest; they are intercon-necting ganglia of images which sometimes reinforce, sometimes oppose, but which always illuminate, each other.

Dostoevsky's works contain two clusters of religious imagery, the more important of the two relating to Christianity, while the other springs from Slavic folklore. Christian imagery in Dostoevsky often overlaps with the tyrant-victim system, since the inversion of the dominance hierarchy is a version of the Christian drama of salvation, incorporating important ele-ments of the passion of Christ. As indicated above in Chapter 8, the importance of crime as a prerequisite to salvation distinguishes Dostoev-sky's system from a strictly Christian concept of salvation and shows that the paradigm dramatizes rite of passage as much as Christian salvation. This brings us into the realm of primitive religion viewed from an anthro-pological perspective, a topic treated at length in the preceding pages. Images from Slavic mythology appear in Dostoevsky, but more important is the general sense in which aggression and subsequent role reversal play a central part in some sort of initiation rite, both on an individual level and in the collective. Psychological and historical-biographical clusters of im-agery thus come into play. The latter has been discussed at length by Hol-quist (who agrees with the above analysis in seeing *Totem and Taboo* as crucial for an understanding of *The Brothers Karamazov*), the former by a host of critics and psychologists. Further, the tyrant-victim paradigm pro-vides an important insight into the Dostoevskian system of social and polit-ical imagery, as is indicated in the previous chapter. Finally, a system of familial imagery, particularly in the last two novels, overlaps with both the psychological and social image clusters and provides a background for the tyrant-victim drama of the late works. None of these systems of imagery has primacy in Dostoevsky; it is the network, not only of related images, but of related image systems, which unifies Dostoevsky's work thematically and structurally. The network is both complex and vast. The preceding pages have attempted to clarify one of its important configurations: Dosto-evsky's peculiar view of the way in which human beings dominate and submit to each other, and define their identities through such acts of domi-nance and submission. By examining this configuration we illuminate the other systems as well. Since dominance and aggression are universal phe-nomena of grave and increasing concern, Dostoevsky's works, and particu-larly this aspect of these works, always remain current. His understanding of these problems provides an important key to our understanding of mod-ern man.

NOTES

Chapter 1: Introduction

[1] Viewed in this light, Dostoevsky's prison memoirs may be seen as a variant of the ethnological tradition in literature, harking back to writers like Chateaubriand, Byron, Rousseau and, in the Russian tradition, Pushkin, Lermontov, Gogol and Marlinsky.

[2] See Joseph Frank, *Dostoevsky: The Seeds of Revolt, 1821–1849* (Princeton: Princeton University Press, 1976), pp. 70–71. Dostoevsky is not a unique observer of this phenomenon. Leskov, to name an example, uses a similar image in "The Left-handed Craftsman." It is Dostoevsky's manner of describing the pecking order, outlined in the following chapters, that is unique.

[3] See René Girard's discussion of this phenomenon in *Violence and the Sacred,* trans. Patrick Gregory (Baltimore: Johns Hopkins University Press, 1977), pp. 94–5.

[4] Andre Gide, *Dostoevsky* (Norfolk, Conn.: New Directions, 1961) pp. 86–88.

[5] See N. K. Mikhailovsky, *Dostoevsky: A Cruel Talent,* trans. Spencer Cadmus (Ann Arbor: Ardis, 1978). Other psychologists and writers (Ivan Turgenev among them) have noted a sadistic streak in Dostoevsky's creative personality, some of them tracing it to his years in prison. See Maria Kravchenko, *Dostoevsky and the Psychologists* (Amsterdam: Verlag Adolf M. Hakkert, 1978), pp. 42, 106. Sigmund Freud, on the other hand, saw an underlying masochistic personality behind the sadistic displays in Dostoevsky's writings. See "Dostoevsky and Parricide," *The Standard Edition of the Complete Psychological Works,* (hereafter: *SECPW*), vol. 21, trans. James Strachey (London: Hogarth Press), pp. 177–194.

[6] Robert L. Jackson discusses Dostoevsky's interest in creating literary types as a means of depicting, or even helping to reform society. But Jackson notes that Dostoevsky sought to avoid mechanical and superficial character typologies. See Robert L. Jackson, Dostoevsky's *Quest for Form* (New Haven: Yale University Press, 1966), pp. 92–123 (esp. pp. 98–9). See also *The Diary of a Writer,* 1873, "In Disguise."

[7] René Girard, *Dostoïevsky: du double à l'unite* (Paris: Librarie Plon, 1963). pp. 19–20.

[8] J. M. Meijer, "Situation Rhyme in a Novel of Dostoevsky," *Dutch Contributions to the Fourth International Congress of Slavists* (The Hague: Mouton, 1958), pp. 115–128.

[9] Ralph Matlaw, "Recurrent Imagery in Dostoevsky," *Harvard Slavic Studies,* vol. 3 (Cambridge, Mass.: Harvard University Press, 1957), pp. 201–225.

Chapter 2: Bonding Hierarchies in Literature before Dostoevsky

[1] Lionel Tiger, *Men in Groups* (New York: Random House, 1969), pp. 18–40, 47–8. Tiger's book has been controversial, to be sure, but most of the criticisms focus on its eclecticism (and on its alleged sexism, a political charge which misunderstands the thesis and says nothing about its scholarly value). Eclecticism is not necessarily a fault in a study dealing with materials which usually fall into the cracks between disciplines. Indeed, most of the reviewers, after nodding in the direction of the purity

of discrete disciplines, concede that Tiger has done a creditable job of bridging gaps which must be bridged. See, for example, *Annals of the American Academy of Political and Social Sciences,* vol. 393 (Jan., 1971), p. 185, *The American Anthropologist,* vol. 72 (Aug., 1970), p. 869, *The New York Times Book Review,* July 27, 1969, p. 10, *The Nation,* vol. 209 (Sept. 22, 1969), p. 286.

[2]Tiger, *op. cit.,* pp. 144, 183.

[3]Tiger, *op. cit.,* p. 134.

[4]See Gary Cox, "Dramatic Imagery as a Tool of Characterization in Lermontov's *A Hero of Our Time,*" *Russian Literature* (Amsterdam), XI-II (Feb., 1982), pp. 163–172.

[5]For an elaboration of Lermontov's and particularly Pechorin's role in the development of Russian psychological realism, see Lidiya Ginzburg, *Tvorcheskii put Lermontova* (Leningrad, 1940).

[6]Donald Fanger, *Dostoevsky and Romantic Realism* (Cambridge, Mass.: Harvard University Press, 1965), pp. 17–18.

[7]Leonid Grossman, *Balzac and Dostoevsky,* trans., Lena Karpov (Ann Arbor: Ardis, 1973).

[8]Honore de Balzac, *Old Goriot,* trans. Marion Ayton Crawford (Baltimore: Penguin Books, 1951), p. 55. Further page references will be parenthesized in the text.

[9]Grossman, *op. cit.,* pp. 33–9, 43–4.

[10]In Tolstoy's "Father Sergius" the competition between a brilliant young officer and his adored tsar over a woman presents a typical Dostoevskian triangle between role model, protege and the woman they both desire. This situation is only the starting point of Tolstoy's story, however, and he goes on to portray the officer's renunciation of that competition and the inward struggles which follow.

Likewise, in Turgenev's nóvel *Smoke,* Potugin's analysis of Russia's relationship with the West may be seen in terms of competition for dominance and the resulting insecurity.

Chapter 3:   The Emotional Solipsist

[1]Lionel Tiger, *Men in Groups* (New York: Random House, 1969), pp. 18–40.

[2]Sigmund Freud, *Group Psychology and the Analysis of the Ego,* pp. 69–143, *SECPW,* vol. XVIII, pp. 95–115.

[3]Tiger, *op. cit.,* p. 135.

[4]René Girard, *Deceit, Desire and the Novel,* trans. Yvonne Freccaro (Baltimore: Johns Hopkins University Press, 1965), pp. 2–3, 9–10.

[5]See Girard's own discussion of Freud in "The Underground Critics," pp. 30–60 in *To Double Business Bound: Essays in Literature, Mimesis and Anthropology* (Baltimore: Johns Hopkins University Press, 1978). pp. 54–5.

[6]George Lukács, "Dostoevsky," pp. 146–158 in *Dostoevsky: A Collection of Critical Essays,* trans. and ed. René Welleck (Englewood Cliffs: Prentice-Hall, 1962), p. 150.

[7]Note the term *"pri mne"* ('except myself'). This is a very odd way of putting it. Literally it means "in my presence" or "in my time," and it is the term used with rulers to denote "during the reign of."

[8]A number of scholars have noted the "solipsism" of this character. This material is introduced here, not because it breaks new ground, but because it provides essential background for arguments forwarded later in the present study. For further discussion of "solipsism" in Dostoevsky's works, see Robert L. Jackson, *Dostoevsky's Underground Man in Russian Literature* (The Hague: Mouton, 1958), pp. 34–36, the same author's *Dostoevsky's Quest for Form* (New Haven: Yale University Press, 1966), p. 6–8; P. M. Bitsilli, "K voprosu o vnutrennei forme romana Dostoevskogo" and "De Sad, Laklo i Dostoevskii," reprinted in *O Dostoevskom: Stati,* ed. Donald Fanger (Providence: Brown University Press, 1966), pp. 38–40, 59–62; and Vyacheslav Ivanov, *Freedom and the Tragic Life* (NY: Noonday Press, 1957), p. 30.

[9]Bernard J. Paris has analyzed *Notes from Underground* from the perspective of Horneyan psychology. He outlines three basic neurotic defense mechanisms: detachment, self-effacement and aggression. The underground man's posture, he maintains, is primarily one of detachment, with occasional forays into aggression and self-effacement. See his article "*Notes from Underground:* A Horneyan Analysis," *PMLA* 88:3 (May 1973), pp. 511–513.

[10]Joseph Frank suggests a connection between this passage and Fyodor Dostoevsky's own adolescent years in the St. Petersburg academy of the military corps of engineers. Biographical documents show that the atmosphere at that school was similar to the one described here. See Joseph Frank, *op. cit.,* pp. 76–7. Arkady Dolgoruky in *A Raw Youth* has comparable schoolboy experiences and, although he is much younger than the underground man, he resembles him in several psychological details. He gets himself thrown out of a tavern at one point and experiences solipsistic feelings several times (See *A Raw Youth,* II 9 I).

[11]The Soviet scholar R. N. Poddubnaya has perceptively outlined the parallels between *Notes from Underground* and "The Shot" (and also Lermontov's *the Masked Ball*). See R. N. Poddubnaya, "Geroi i ego literaturnoe razvitie," pp. 54–66 in *Dostoevsky: Materialy i issledovaniya,* ed. G. M. Fridlender (Leningrad: Izdatelstvo "Nauka," 1978), pp. 55–57.

[12]P. M. Bitsilli has noted another similarity with the *Divine Comedy* in terms of narrative technique. In both Dostoevsky's and Dante's works, he says, a neutral and impersonal narrator acts as the reader's guide. See P. M. Bitsilli, "Pochemu Dostoevsky ne napisal *Zhitiya velikago greshnika*?" pp. 25–30 in *O Dostoevskom,* vol. 2, ed. A. L. Bem (Prague, 1933).

[13]See E. N. Opochinin, "Besedy s Dostoevskim," pp. 454–494 in *Zvenya,* vol. 6 (Moscow: Academia, 1936), p. 457.

[14]See Frank, *op. cit.,* pp. 160–169; A. Ya. Panaeva, "Iz vospominaniya," in *F. M. Dostoevsky v vospominaniyakh sovremennikov,*" (Moscow: Izdatelstvo 'Khudozhestvennaya literatura,' 1964), pp. 140–44.

Chapter 4:   Identity Crisis and Character Doubling

[1]Mikhail Bakhtin, *Problems of Dostoevsky's Poetics* (Ann Arbor: Ardis, 1973), p. 38.

[2]See Robert Louis Jackson *Dostoevsky's Underground Man in Russian Literature* (The Hague: Mouton, 1958), p. 36.

[3]See Robert Ardrey, *The Social Contract* (NY: Atheneum, 1970) pp. 186, 324–5.

[4]Sigmund Freud, *Civilization and Its Discontents, SECPW* vol. 21, pp. 64–73.

[5]Vyacheslav Ivanov, *Dostoevsky: Freedom and the Tragic Life,* trans. Norman Cameron (NY: Noonday Press, 1957), pp. 26–30.

[6]René Girard, *Deceit, Desire and the Novel,* pp. 54–58; *Dostoïevski: Du double à l'unite,* p. 94.

[7]For a discussion of the relation of sadomasochism to Dostoevskian solipsism, see P. M. Bitsilli "De-Sad (DeSade), Laklo (Laclos) i Dostoevsky" (pp. 58–64 in Donald Fanger, ed., *O Dostoevskom: Stati* (Providence: Brown University Press, 1966). Martin P. Rice relates the struggles of the Dostoevskian self in relation to others to Hegel's concepts of "Master" and "Slave." See Martin P. Rice "Dostoevsky's *Notes from Underground* and Hegel's 'Master and Slave,'" pp. 359–369 in *Canadian–American Slavic Studies* 8:3 (Fall, 1974).

[8]See R. P. Blackmur, *Eleven Essays in the European Novel,* (NY: Harcourt, Brace & World, 1964), p. 130; Richard Peace, *Dostoevsky* (Cambridge: Cambridge University Press, 1971), pp. 35–7; Dmitri Chizhevsky "Dostoevsky—psikholog," in A. S. Bem, ed., *O Dostoevskom: Stati* vol. 2, (Prague, 1933), p. 71; S. Askoldov "Psikhologiya kharakterov Dostoevskogo" in A. S. Dolinin, ed., *Dostoevsky: Stati i materialy.* (Leningrad: Mysl, 1925), pp. 8–24.

[9]See Girard, *Dostoïevski: Du double à l'unite,* pp. 53–4.

[10]See George Steiner, *Tolstoy or Dostoevsky: An Essay in the Old Criticism* (NY: Alfred A. Knopf, 1959), pp. 220.

[11]American poet Sylvia Plath wrote a senior honors thesis at Smith College on the double in Dostoevsky's works. She noted that Golyadkin's death wish "is a severe intensification of his desire to hide in the dark and originates from an acute sense of persecution. See George Gibian "The Theme of the Double, Sylvia Plath and Dostoevsky" pp. 636–42 in *Crime and Punishment* (NY: Norton Critical Edition, 1975).

[12]See Victor Terras *The Young Dostoevsky* (The Hague; Mouton, 1969) p. 181.

[13]A. L. Bem argues that the second Golyadkin is invented to bear the "primordial guilt" that the real Golyadkin feels and to keep that guilt away from his "ideal self." His interpretation takes into account only the negative features of the double and ignores the ways in which he fulfills Golyadkin's ambitions. See A. L. Bem, *Dostoevsky: Psikhoanaliticheskie etyudy* (Prague, 1938) p. 181. Roger Anderson argues more convincingly that Golyadkin and his double represent the passive and assertive images of the self. See Roger B. Anderson, "Dostoevsky's Hero in *The Double:* A Reexamination of Divided Self" pp. 101–113 in *Symposium* XXVI 2 (Summer 1976).

Chapter 5:   The Friend as Enemy

[1]A. L. Bem, *Dostoevsky: Psikhoanaliticheskie etyudy,* pp. 22. Cf. the Jungian concept of the "shadow," an alter ego either within or outside the self, upon which positive or negative qualities are projected. See Esther Harding, *The 'I' and the 'Not-I'* (NY: Pantheon Books, 1965), pp. 76–79.

[2]Compare this with Leslie Fiedler's discussion of similar love-hate bonds between male characters in American literature, e.g., Chillingworth and Dimmesdale, Claggart and Billy Budd. See Leslie Fiedler, *Love and Death in the American Novel* (NY: Stein and Day, 1960).

[3]A number of critics have commented on the fundamental opposition between these two characters, beginning with D. H. Lawrence and J. Middleton Murry. They disagreed on this issue, Lawrence seeing this cosmic opposition in sexual terms, Murry seeing it in spiritual terms. Their disagreement on this issue seems to have been a prelude to the personal rift between them, and, indeed, their own relationship seems to have embodied a dynamic not unlike the Rogozhin/Myshkin doubling. In any case they had planned to write a book on Dostoevsky together, but gave up the project and wrote separate books. For further discussion of this topic, see Gary Cox, "F. M. Dostoevsky and D. H. Lawrence: Mirror Images of Murderous Aggression," in *Modern Fiction Studies,* 29 (1983): 2. See also D. H. Lawrence, "The Crown," in *Reflections on the Death of a Porcupine* (Bloomington, Indiana: Indiana Univesity Press, 1963), pp. 55–56; J. M. Murry, *Fyodor Dostoevsky: A Critical Study* (NY: Dodd, Mead and Co., 1916) pp. 152–3; J. M. Murry *Reminiscences of .D H. Lawrence* (NY: H. Holt and Co., 1933). See also Robert Lord, *Dostoevsky: Essays and Perspectives* (Berkeley: University of California Press, 1970) p. 98; Alex de Jonge, *Dostoevsky and the Age of Intensity* (NY: St. Martin's Press, 1975) pp. 117–18.

[4]The name "Rogozhin," although derived from *rogozha* ('bast mat'), also suggests *rog* ('horn,' 'antler'), implying masculine aggressiveness. It may also link him with the "Rogozhskaya" section of Moscow, noted for its Old Believer church.

[5]Robin Miller notes that both Myshkin and Rogozhin resemble the Gothic hero or villain in that they are cut off from the beauties of the universe available to the normal man. See Robin Miller, *The Multi-Voiced Narrator of 'The Idiot,'* Columbia University Dissertation, 1977, p. 179.

[6]"Kenotic" is a term widely used in Greek Orthodox theology to describe Christ's self-abnegating sacrifice of his divine attributes in order to redeem mankind. See George P. Fedotov, *The Russian Religious Mind* (Cambridge, Mass.: Harvard University Press, 1946) pp. 94–131. Myshkin's name also combines opposites with regard to the dominance hierarchy. His last name is based on *mysh* ('mouse'), but his first name, Lyov, means 'lion.' Simon D. Lesser interprets Myshkin's "kenotic" behavior in less positive fashion, as straightforward masochism. See "Saint and Sinner in Dostoevsky's 'Idiot'" pp. 211–224. *Modern Fiction Studies* 4 (1958) 3.

[7]Malcom Jones notes that these contrasting physical objects symbolize their relationship. *Dostoevsky: The Novel of Discord* (NY: Barnes and Noble, 1976) p. 103.

[8]See Sigmund Freud, *The Interpretation of Dreams,* vol. 1, *SECPW,* vol. 4, pp. 134–162 for a discussion of such distortion and "censorship" in dreams.

[9]In his article on Dostoevsky, Freud notes the psychological connection between epilepsy and coitus. "Dostoevsky and Parricide," *SECPW,* vol. 21, pp. 81–3.

[10]Lionel Tiger, along similar lines, notes that a female may act as a "catalyst" in the formation of male bonds, especially when symbolic behavior is involved. See Tiger, *op. cit.,* p. 124.

[11]In some ways this character, embracing so many extremes, seems to be a rough sketch for Stavrogin or Versilov. See F. M. Dostoevsky, *Polnoe sobranie sochinenii* (hereafter: *PSS*), vol. 7 (Leningrad: Nauka, 1972–1981), p. 141; R. P. Blackmur, *Eleven Essays in the European Novel,* (NY: Harcourt Brace and World, 1964) p. 159.

[12]Elizabeth Dalton, *Unconscious Structure in 'The Idiot': A Study in Literature and Psychoanalysis* (Princeton: Princeton University Press, 1979) pp. 90–93, 112.

[13]Girard himself admits this in "The Underground Critic," pp. 36–60 in *To Double Business Bound* pp. 54–5. In another sense, of course, Myshkin acts as the mediator or model for practically everyone in the novel, as Robin Miller has noted. See Robin Miller, *op. cit.,* p. 380.

[14]See F. M. Dostoevsky, *PSS* 7, pp. 21, 43, emphasis Dostoevsky's.

[15]Ippolit's position in the novel is complex. His protege relationship with Myshkin reminds us of Alyosha Karamazov and Kolya Krasotkin, but he also has an adolescent fascination with Rogozhin (III 6) which parallels Myshkin's bond with that character. He says in his "Explanation" that he both envies and resents Rogozhin's power, which reminds him of a huge spider. (III 6) Not only do characters double each other in Dostoevsky, but those very doublings are echoed by other pairings.

[16]See René Girard, *Dostoïevski: Du double à l'unite* pp. 30–37.

[17]For further discussion of this aspect of *Netochka Nezvanova,* see Victor Terras, *op. cit.,* p. 105; and Joseph Frank, *op. cit.,* p. 359.

[18]For further discussion of these letters, see Richard Peace *Dostoevsky* (Cambridge: Cambridge University Press, 1971), pp. 107–8.

[19]See Richard Peace, *op. cit.,* pp. 35–7. For further discussion of the phenomenon of doubling in Dostoevsky's novels, see works listed in Chapter 4, note 8.

[20]To be sure, the symbol is not this simple, for from another point of view Stepan Verkhovensky may be seen as this demoniac. Typical of symbolism in Dostoevsky, the parable of the demoniac and the swine reverberates with alternative meanings in this novel.

[21]Irving Howe sees Kirillov and Shatov as split halves of a hypothetical self, living as they do in the same house, yet intellectually isolated and incomplete without Stavrogin. See "Dostoevsky: The Politics of Salvation" in *Dostoevsky: A Collection of Critical Essays* (Englewood Cliffs, NJ: Prentice-Hall, 1962) pp. 63–4.

[22]See *PSS* XI, 63; Edward Wasiolek *The Notebooks for 'The Possessed,'* (Chicago: University of Chicago Press, 1968), p. 76.

Chapter 6:   The Lover as Tyrant

[1]Quoted in E. N. Opochinin, *op. cit.,* pp. 462–3.

[2]George Steiner, *Tolstoy or Dostoevsky: An Essay in the Old Criticism* (NY: Alfred A. Knopf, 1959), p. 201. See also Thomas G. Masaryk, *The Spirit of Russia,* vol. 3, trans. Robert Bass (NY: Barnes and Nobel, 1967), pp. 88–90.

[3]A. L. Bem sees this structure as related to Dostoevsky's relationship with his parents. *Dostoevsky: Psikhoanaliticheskie etyudy,* p. 117. An interesting analysis of these structures in Dostoevsky's own romantic life may be found in Marc Slonim, *Three Loves of Dostoevsky* (NY: Rinehart and Co., 1955). It is interesting that the works concerned with the *menage à trois* were written early in Dostoevsky's career, a period when the author himself was involved in such triangular relationships with older women (his first wife) or aggressive women (Polina Suslova), while the interest in straightforward domination of younger women by older men is clearer in the late period, when Dostoevsky was happily married to a woman young enough to be his daughter. Such considerations are not really germane to this study, however.

[4]One of the artistic deficiencies of the work is the lack of data for evaluating her character, her emotions, or the motives for her suicide. Her death forms the climax of the work, and since we see her only from the narrator's decidedly strange viewpoint, we have no more idea than he does about the reasons for her suicide. This leaves the reader with a dissatisfying sense of confusion, since we have good reason to doubt the validity of his perceptions.

[5]In the rough drafts both Dunya and Sonya have more characteristics of the proud "infernal woman," resembling Nastasya Filippovna in their combination of passivity and aggressiveness. See *PSS* 7, pp. 152–6; Edward Wasiolek, *The Notebooks for 'Crime and Punishment,'* (Chicago: University of Chicago Press), pp. 44–47, 191.

[6]See *PSS* 7, p. 80; Wasiolek *The Notebooks for 'Crime and Punishment,'* p. 96.

[7]Richard Peace, *op. cit.,* pp. 35–37.

[8]In a sense he identifies with his other victim (the pawnbroker) as well, when he calls her a louse, and says that he killed her to prove that he was not a louse. (V 4)

[9]See R. P. Blackmur, *op. cit.,* p. 133.

Chapter 7:   Guilt, compassion, and the Power of Weakness

[1]This word is the only one italicized in the entire chapter. It is also italicized in "A Gentle Girl."

[2]See P. M. Bitsilli, "K voprosu o vnutrennei forme romana Dostoevskogo," in *O Dostoevskom: Stati,* ed. Donald Fanger (Providence: Brown University Press, 1966), p. 40.

[3]Even General Ivolgin's fabricated story about his childhood influence on Napoleon exhibits this structure, although on another level it is pure humbug (*vranyo*) and functions merely as a comic-pathetic interlude. He alleges that Napoleon took an interest in him upon finding out that his father had died defending Moscow, and came to value the boy's advice over that of his own aides. (IV 4)

[4]Sigmund Freud, *Totem and Taboo,* vol. 13, *SECPW,* pp. 100–139.

[5]Sigmund Freud, *Group Psychology and the Analysis of the Ego,* vol. 18, *SECPW,* p. 124.

[6]René Girard, *Violence and the Sacred,* pp. 94–95, 202–3; Mikhail Bakhtin, *op. cit.,* pp. 162–176.

[7]See Dalton, *op. cit.,* pp. 73–5.

[8]This pattern of police power in the guise of weakness has even become a staple of the detective novel tradition. Porfiry Petrovich has a host of literary descendants: brilliant detectives whom no one would suspect of being capable of such a calling. Beginning with the reclusive violinist and cocaine addict Sherlock Holmes, the tradition includes a mild-mannered priest in G. K. Chesterton's Father Brown stories and a good natured maiden-aunt in Agatha Christie's Miss Marple. Christie's greatest detective, the fussy and delicate Frenchman Hercule Poirot, resembles Porfiry Petrovich even in appearance, and even his name contains a paradoxical reference to his power. The television detective Columbo uses a technique so similar to Porfiry Petrovich's that one suspects actual imitation. The secret power of weakness is not only an important part of Dostoevsky's catalog of human behavior; it has become a part of the literary tradition.

Chapter 8:   The Criminal as Victim

[1]See Richard Peace, *op. cit.,* pp. 180–83, and Andre Gide, *op. cit.,* pp. 104–5.

[2]René Girard relates Stavrogin's problems to his own concept of mimetic desire. Stavrogin, he says, represents a type of masochism in which the master or mediator, having realized that the object of desire is a void, wills his own failure, and does so by seeking an object which is denied by an insurmountable obstacle. *Deceit, Desire and the Novel,* p. 176.

[3]See *PSS* 11 63; Edward Wasiolek, *The Notebooks for 'The Possessed',* pp. 54, 68.

[4]P. N. Bitsilli, for instance, has noted a peculiar absence of personality in Stavrogin which makes this character easy to parody. "Pochemu Dostoevsky ne napisal zhitiya velikago greshnika," p. 27.

[5]Michael Cherniavsky has noted a similar combination of dominant and victimized characteristics in the Slavophile doctrine of the Christlike tsar, whose power is a burden shouldered for the redemption of his people. *Tsar and People: Studies in Russian Myths* (New Haven: Yale University Press, 1961), p. 184.

[6]Sigmund Freud "Dostoevsky and Parricide," vol. 21, *SECPW,* pp. 189–90. Lev Shestov also notes that criminality is a positive ideal in Dostoevsky's late works. The writer is making an obeisance to the convicts he knew during his prison years, even though they had despised him. *Dostoevsky, Tolstoy and Nietzsche,* trans. Spencer Roberts, (Columbus, Ohio: Ohio University Press, 1969), pp. 211–12. Other critics, although not going quite this far, have noticed the special status of the criminal in the late works of Dostoevsky. See D. S. Merezhkovsky, "Besnovaty ili prorok," in *Prorok russkoi revolyutsii* (St. Petersburg: Pirozhkov, 1906, pp. 63–77, and Donald Fanger, *op. cit.,* p. 37.

[7]René Girard, *Dostoïevski: Du double à l'unite,* pp. 116–117.

Chapter 9:   Primal Murders

[1]See Edward Wasiolek, *Dostoevsky: The Major Fiction* (Cambridge, Mass.: M.I.T. Press, 1964), pp. 156–8.

[2]See Michael Holquist, *Dostoevsky and the Novel,* (Princeton: Princeton University Press, 1977), pp. 189.

[3]*The Brothers Karamazov* is linked with *Crime and Punishment* in a special way. They are Dostoevsky's best full length novels, and the only ones in which his drama of redemption is completed. In both of these novels the progression from violent crime, through pity and guilt, to redemption is also a rite of passage from adolescence to adulthood. The preface to *The Brothers Karamazov* suggests interesting connections between the two novels. Here we are told that this novel is a preface to another novel (this was also suggested in the final sentence of the epilogue of *Crime and Punishment*) and that the events recorded in *The Brothers Karamazov* happened thirteen years before its writing, that is, in 1867, the year *Crime and Punishment* was finished. Since the year 1867 was a crucial transitional year in Dostoevsky's personal and professional life (it was the year of his successful marriage and of a radical change for the better in his professional fortunes) it is possible that these fictional treatments of the rite of passage were linked with changes in Dostoevsky's own life. See Malcom Jones, *Dostoevsky: The Novel of Discord* (New York: Barnes and Noble, 1976), pp. 171.

[4]Dostoevsky's novel does not appear to have been a conscious source of Freud's anthropological theory, however. In fact, Freud's article on Dostoevsky is disappointing. He is more interested in Dostoevsky as a case study supporting Oedipal theory than as a thinker or artist. He spends most of the article trying to establish a connection between Dostoevsky's epilepsy and the murder of his father by a group of peasants (sometimes with flimsy evidence) and talking about the link between gambling and masturbation. See Sigmund Freud, "Dostoevsky and Parricide," in *SECPW,* vol. 21, pp. 175.

[5]Sigmund Freud, *Totem and Taboo,* vol. 13, *SECPW,* pp. 143.

[6]Robin Fox points out that most of the objections to the theory sprang from Freud's incorrect assumption that gorillas stood in the direct line of hominid evolution. Fox observes that family structures similar to those of Freud's "primal horde" are typical of baboons as well, and argues that such baboon-like structures would have been adaptive for proto-hominid groups as they moved from forest to savannah. He also argues that the primal murder need not have actually taken place in order to be important in human cultural evolution. The impulse to such action may have contributed to the development of initiation rites as a way of averting the primal murder. See Robin Fox, "In the Beginning: Aspects of Hominid Behavioral Evolution," pp. 415–433 in *Man* 2:3 (September, 1967); and M. R. A. Chance and Alan Mead, "Social Behavior and Primate Evolution," in *Evolution,* vol. 7 of *Symposia of the Society for Experimental Biology* (NY: Jonathan Cape, 1953).

[7]Michael Holquist has noted the connection between *The Brothers Karamazov* and Freud's *Totem and Taboo,* but he does not elaborate on the ritual nature of the deaths of Ilyusha and Fyodor Pavlovich. His idea of "sons becoming Fathers," suggests the inversion of the dominance hierarchy outlined above. Holquist, *op. cit.,* pp. 177–181.

[8]Geoffrey Kabat, *op. cit.,* pp. 118.

[9]This subplot also parallels quite closely the story of Swiss Marie in *The Idiot.* (I 6) In other ways this group crime echoes the murder of Shatov in *The Devils,* but there the sense of guilt is totally lacking, so the crime has no redemptive impact.

[10]See *PSS* XV, pp. 306; and Edward Wasiolek, *The Notebooks for 'The Brothers Karamazov'* (Chicago: University of Chicago Press, 1971), pp. 186–7.

[11]Vyacheslav Ivanov and A. K. Gornostaev have noted that the death of Ilyusha becomes a foundation for religious consciousness in the boys, and Gornostaev connects these apsects of *The Brothers Karamazov* with Nikolai Fyodorov's utopian ideas on the resurrection of ancestors. Dostoevsky was reading Fyodorov during the late 1870's and was in substantial agreement with some of his ideas. See A. K. Gornostaev, *Rai na zemle* (Kharbin, 1929), pp. 37–40, 65–66; and Stephen Lukashevich, *N. F. Fyodorov: A Study in Russian Eupsychian and Utopian Thought* (Newark, Delaware: University of Delaware Press, 1977), pp. 20–21.

[12]Lionel Tiger has observed that guilt is related to male bonding as an important cohesive force in primitive human social behavior. See *Men in Groups,* p. 48.

[13]René Girard, *Violence and the Sacred,* pp. 4–6, 26, 197–8.

[14]René Girard, "The Underground Critic," pp. 56. See also George Steiner, *op. cit.,* p. 204.

[15]See Erich Fromm, *The Anatomy of Human Destructiveness,* (Greenwich, Conn: Fawcett Crest, 1973), pp. 323, for a discussion of similar compensatory mechanisms in sadistic individuals.

Chapter 10:   The Dominance Hierarchy in Political Behavior

[1]For further elaboration of this aspect of Dostoevsky's work see the author's article "Dostoevskian Psychology and Russian Cultural and Political Identity," forthcoming in *Mosaic: A Journal for the Interdisciplinary Study of Literature*, XVII 3..

[2]From an article in *Time* (*Vremya*). See David Magarshack, *Dostoevsky's Occasional Writings* (New York: Random House, 1963), pp. 75.

[3]See also G. M. Fridlender, "Estetika Dostoevskogo," pp. 97–164 in *Dostoevsky: Khudozhnik i myslitel: Sbornik statei* (Moscow: Khudozhestvennaya literatura, 1972), pp. 106.

[4]". . . like some arrogant dude (*fert*) with his hands on his hips, spitting contemptuously. . . ." this very image was used in *Notes from Underground,* published at about same time, to characterize the hostility of the laws of nature toward the underground man. According to Geoffrey Kabat, the image of parents abandoning children also implicitly represents the gentry's abandonment of the peasantry. See Geoffrey Kabat, *op. cit.,* pp. 117.

[5]Lev Shestov, *op. cit.,* pp. 211–12.

[6]Nikolai Berdyaev, *Dostoevsky* (London: Sheed and Ward, 1934), pp. 167–8.

[7]D. H. Lawrence,"Preface to Dostoevsky's 'Grand Inquisitor,'" pp. 90–97 in *Dostoevsky: A Collection of Critical Essays,* ed. René Welleck (Englewood cliffs, N.J., 1962).

Chapter 11:   The Structure of Dostoevsky's Images

[1]Robin Miller uses the image of the kaleidoscope to describe the "multi-voiced" narration of *The Idiot.* See Robin Miller, *op. cit.*

[2]The term is J. M. Meijer's. See "Situation Rhyme," pp. 116.

[3]See Meijer, *op. cit.,* pp. 120.

[4]See Matlaw, "Recurrent Imagery," pp. 204–9.